PRAISE FOR *RETURN OF*

"*Return of the Condor* is an account of cutting-edge conservation biology, but it is also an eminently human story. John Moir's focus is on the problematic intersection between science and scientists, between bird lovers and the great bird itself. The subject matter—complex and controversial, ultimately heartwarming—demands a skilled and sympathetic writer, and Moir's chronicle is thoroughly successful in this regard."

—Ted Floyd, editor of *Birding* magazine,
American Birding Association

"Moir deftly chronicles the efforts of the dedicated biologists . . . who work to save the California condor from extinction."

—*Publishers Weekly*

"Highly recommended."

—*Library Journal*

"With eloquence and insight, John Moir chronicles the effort to save this spectacular bird. His book is a remarkable testament to what a few dedicated individuals can accomplish."

—Tim Gallagher, director of publications,
Cornell Laboratory of Ornithology

"Moir, whose prize-winning story for *Birding* magazine grew into this book, tells of the salvation of the condor."

—*Booklist*

"John Moir's dramatic account of bringing the condor back from the brink of extinction is a reminder of the fragility of life on our planet and of the capacity of one species, humans, to protect or extinguish all others. *Return of the Condor* is a powerful tribute to the scientists, politicians, hunters, environmentalists, and concerned citizens who ultimately found a way to work together to ensure the survival of one of the most remarkable species on Earth."

—Mark Schaefer, CEO, Global Environment and Technology Foundation; former president of NatureServe

"The story grips our attention as a good novel does and will be enjoyed by birders, environmentalists, and curious laymen alike."

—*Wildbird* magazine

"Pulling the California condor back from the brink of extinction has been difficult, and expensive. But this fine book by John Moir makes abundantly clear why preserving magnificent beings like our once-more wild condors is one of twenty-first-century society's more important obligations."

—Alan Tennant, author of *On the Wing: To the Edge of the Earth with the Peregrine Falcon*

"A riveting, readable story of a bird's rescue."

—*Midwest Book Review*

"John Moir has written an uplifting and well-researched tale that takes us on the condor's roller-coaster ride to recovery. Equally exhilarating and heartbreaking, this important story brings complex issues into clear focus and lets us understand—with both heart and mind—why we need to save this intelligent and majestic bird."

—Maria Mudd Ruth, author of *Rare Bird: Pursuing the Mystery of the Marbled Murrelet*

RETURN OF THE CONDOR

THE RACE TO SAVE
OUR LARGEST BIRD FROM EXTINCTION

O

JOHN MOIR

LYONS
PRESS

Essex, Connecticut

An imprint of Globe Pequot, the trade division of
The Rowman & Littlefield Publishing Group, Inc.
4501 Forbes Blvd., Ste. 200
Lanham, MD 20706
www.rowman.com

Distributed by NATIONAL BOOK NETWORK

British Library Cataloguing in Publication Information available

Library of Congress Cataloging-in-Publication Data available
ISBN 978-1-4930-7665-9 (paper : alk. paper)
ISBN 978-1-4930-7875-2 (electronic)

Printed in India

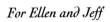

For Ellen and Jeff

CONTENTS

Contents

ACKNOWLEDGMENTS

MY THANKS TO the newspaper and magazine editors, including *Birding* magazine editor Ted Floyd, who helped give birth to this book by indulging my passion to write about a gigantic, nearly extinct vulture.

I am immensely grateful for my agent—and fellow birder—Robert Shepard. Robert's early support was crucial, and his invaluable insights into the book's narrative structure helped shape the manuscript. Moreover, his wisdom, optimism, and friendship are a true gift. Special thanks also go to Ruth Greenstein, an extraordinary wordsmith. Ruth used her intelligence and good humor to sprinkle magic over my words. At Lyons Press, I greatly appreciated the support and enthusiasm of my editor, Lilly Golden, and her excellent staff. And, for their work on the book's new edition, my appreciation and thanks to Eugene Brissie and Meredith Dias.

This book would not exist without the generosity of so many people affiliated with the condor recovery effort. I am especially indebted to Jan Hamber for her assistance and support (and for always having a chocolate bar handy). In addition, my thanks to the following: Noel and Helen Snyder, Bill Toone, Fred Sibley, Jesse Grantham, Phil Ensley, Pete Bloom, Steve Kimple, John Ogden, Bill Heinrich, Dave Clendenen, Nora Toth, Mark Hall, Denise Stockton, Lisa Drake, Susie Kasielke, Debbie Sears, Sheila Foster, Grainger Hunt, Paul Andreano, Anthony Prieto, Chris Parish, Allan Mee,

Kelly Sorenson, Mike Mace, Mike Wallace, Cynthia Stringfield, Jack Cafferty, Gregg Austin, Joe Burnett, Myra Finkelstein, Tiana Williams-Claussen, Ashleigh Blackford, Samantha Gibbs, and Steve Kirkland.

Thanks also to the following people who helped me in researching this story: Carla Cicero, Karen Klitz, and Julie Woodruff at the Museum of Vertebrate Zoology at UC Berkeley; Peter Capainolo at the American Museum of Natural History; Gary Robinson and the staff at the Santa Barbara Museum of Natural History; Brett Dickerson, U.S. Fish & Wildlife Service; U.S. Attorney Bob Wright; Charlie McLaughlin and Rick Throckmorton at Aspen Helicopters; Greg and Linda McMillan of Cholame, California; and writers Ken Brower and Tom Burnett. My appreciation also goes to the staff at the Los Angeles Zoo, the San Diego Zoo's Wild Animal Park, the Peregrine Fund, the Ventana Wildlife Society, and the U.S. Fish & Wildlife Service.

During the long journey to publication, many people inspired and supported me, including Joe Cook and Marina Cook, Jim and Melinda Moir, Larry Rosen, Cliff and Sara Friedlander, Jeannie Herrick, Mike Knowles, Ellen Wood, Rosemary Faitos, Jeanne Lance, Clay Madden, Todd Newberry, Kay Murphy, Tim Kelly, Eric Maisel, Seena Frost, Heidi Rentería, Ron Wingard, and Leslie Tremaine. Also, a remembrance for three exceptional people who are no longer with us: Lynn Petrock, Jeff Merrill, and Tom Cuthbertson.

In addition, my thanks to the eMSS staff, the New Teacher Project, and everyone at the Elkhorn Slough National Estuarine Research Reserve (the Cosmic Center of the Universe). Special appreciation to Insight Santa Cruz. And to my literary coconspirators, the MOBsters, my gratitude for all the conversations and camaraderie.

I am forever grateful to my parents, who encouraged my love of nature and stories. To Jeff and Kimberly and their boys, Desmond and Miles: you fill each day with love and happiness. And to my wife, Ellen: my first editor, my lifelong companion, the kindest person I know—you are the wind beneath my wings.

INTRODUCTION

AN HOUR'S DRIVE north of Los Angeles's freeways and cement-colored skies lies the Sespe Condor Sanctuary—a fifty-three-thousand acre wilderness area that hasn't changed much in ten thousand years. In the mid-1970s, I spent two years living in nearby Santa Paula, a pastoral town just east of Ventura nestled among the orange groves of the Santa Clara River Valley. The sanctuary is part of the mountainous Los Padres National Forest, which I could see from my house.

These wild mountains are my kind of place.

Whenever I could get away into the area's remote canyons and cliffs, I always had one eye on the sky for California condors. At the time, however, there were only a few of the birds remaining in the world, and despite many days of hiking and backpacking the chaparral- and pine-covered mountains, I had never seen one.

That changed one windy late-winter day when I took one of my favorite hikes: the steep climb up Santa Paula Peak. I drove to the trailhead east of Santa Paula, clambered over a rusty iron gate, and headed into condor country. Above me towered the formidable summit of five-thousand-foot Santa Paula Peak. After an hour's walk up a dirt road that wound through citrus and avocado orchards, I arrived at the edge of the Los Padres National Forest. Far above, floating in another world, turkey vultures and golden eagles circled the peak's crumbling cliffs. The road narrowed into a steep trail that switchbacked up the mountain's shoulder. The wind grew stronger, and as I climbed, thick chaparral pulled at my clothes. Every few minutes I stopped to flick ticks off my jeans.

After several hours of hard climbing I reached the summit. There, I stopped to rest and to eat a sandwich. Despite the wind and gathering clouds, I decided to follow the trail farther north toward the distant peaks of the Topa Topa Mountains. As I picked my way along a narrow ridge, two enormous birds swept over the horizon and hurtled across the sky. They dipped lower, their white wing patches silhouetted in black, and peered down at me, their orange-colored heads unmistakable. The wind howled, but in my memory, I can hear the air whistling through their flight feathers. The birds were gigantic—they looked like small airplanes. These were my first condors.

I scrambled to unpack a pair of binoculars, but the birds dipped their wings and disappeared down a canyon. I waited—hoping—but the condors did not return. As a few drops of rain splashed my jacket, I turned and hiked down the mountain, my euphoria ebbing into the wind. The encounter had been less than two minutes—much too short. And because of the birds' precarious predicament, it was very possible that I might never see another condor again.

○

It turned out I *would* see condors again—many of them—but not before the species nearly vanished. More than two decades of turmoil and trouble passed before I would again have a chance to witness this magnificent bird in flight.

It happened one August day in the mid-1990s. A friend and I drove south from Monterey down the Big Sur coastline, following Highway 1 as it meandered along the edge of the continent. The condor recovery program had just released a handful of birds in the area, and we wanted to see them.

The two-lane highway crossed several creeks via gracefully arched bridges, and skirted a coastline of tumbling cliffs where the

Santa Lucia Mountains plunged into the Pacific. Small rock islands crowded with cormorants dotted the coast. The area abounds with turkey vultures, we soon discovered, which, to the unpracticed eye, resemble condors in flight. We spent several hours chasing "TVs." By mid-afternoon we were at Julia Pfeiffer Burns State Park, where scenic McWay Falls drops eighty feet over a granite precipice into an aqua-green ocean cove. A mile or more inland, we spotted five huge black birds circling a distant hill. Their steady flight and strong flat wings screamed "condor." But the birds were so far away we couldn't be sure. What should we do? We waited another half hour, and then, with doubt eroding any sense of jubilation, we decided to head home.

A mile up the highway we spotted a man with binoculars standing alongside a pickup truck with a rooftop radio antenna. We stopped and asked if he knew where to see condors.

"Sure," he said. "I've got the birds on the radio telemetry right now."

He introduced himself as Joe Burnett, field supervisor for the Ventana Wildlife Society, the group managing the condor releases in Central California. Burnett told us that he thought the condors were headed for a spot a mile or two up the coast. We followed his pickup, and five minutes later we stood in a gravel turnout alongside Highway 1. Burnett's radio clicked—the condors were coming.

The first two birds crested the coastal hills beside the road; three more followed. First through binoculars, and then with our spotting scope, we watched the condors soar. The mythical birds had come home. After a few minutes, I felt lightheaded and realized I was holding my breath.

We spent the next hour talking to Joe Burnett and watching condors. Someday, when I'm an old man, and I look back to count up the good days—the *really* good days that leaven one's life—I shall put on my list that afternoon in Big Sur with black-and-white condors flying through a blue sky.

○

The trip to the Big Sur coast ignited my interest. My background as a birder and science writer led me to spend many more days following the birds. As I began to work on articles about the condor recovery program, team members befriended me. I hiked with them to backcountry flight pens and listened to their tales of persistence and sacrifice.

Their stories hooked me. At first, the tales tugged gently at my curiosity. Eventually they grew into a floodtide that carried me away. They created the momentum that led to this book.

Writer Wade Davis said, "I believe that storytelling changes the world." In following the condor's story, I discovered that this epic is also a saga of human courage and controversy. And I learned that the tales of some of the last wild condors are as compelling as those of their human counterparts.

All of these stories, however, are anchored by the heart-stopping experience of seeing a condor flying overhead: The gigantic bird sweeping across the sky, its wings stretching to an impossible ten feet, white triangular patches on the undersides flashing in the sun, sending shivers up your spine. As it swoops lower, looking down at you with curious eyes, the ordinary world drops away and magic prowls the horizon.

While it is one thing to describe a condor with words or to see a picture, it's quite another to view it soaring through the air. During my research, I've watched people witness the bird in flight for the first time. It's a moment to remember. What happened one spring morning in 2004 is typical. I came upon a group of hikers on a ridge at Pinnacles National Monument.* Several condors had been released in this Central California location just a few months earlier. The hikers were looking at the first bird of the day, perched two hundred yards away on one of Pinnacles' volcanic spires. It didn't look like much—a bun-

---

*In 2013, Pinnacles National Monument was redesignated as Pinnacles National Park.

dle of black feathers hunched on gray stone. The condor then spread its wings and lofted into the air. Several hikers gasped.

"That's amazing," a woman behind me said. The bird wheeled no more than fifty feet overhead, its stunning size and colors on full display. "That's amazing," the woman repeated. As the bird traced lazy circles above us, she said again, "That's amazing." Ten minutes later, softer now, still unaware she was speaking aloud, she continued her mantra for the flying condor: "That's amazing."

If you listen carefully as a condor passes close overhead, you can sometimes hear the air whistle through its flight feathers. This wind song of the condor is the music of hope. Hope that America's largest bird will once again fly free, without the shackles of number tags and radio transmitters. Hope that by preserving the condor we open the way for protecting less majestic but equally vital species from extinction. Hope that our children and grandchildren may one day enjoy the flight of the condor. Hope that by saving this ancient bird, we can save ourselves.

1

The Last Condor

JAN HAMBER FACED an agonizing dilemma. The California condor she had been tracking—the last member of its species to exist in the wild—had approached a trap site on the remote Hudson Ranch just north of Los Angeles. It was late on a spring day in 1987, and Jan watched through her binoculars as AC9 (Adult Condor 9) landed near the stillborn calf that served as bait. He circled the carcass, keeping his distance, while a golden eagle fed on the calf. The sunlight accented AC9's intelligent eyes and bare, salmon-colored head. An ink-black ruff of feathers circled the base of his neck. AC9 stretched and refolded his wings, and as the sun sank lower over the chaparral-covered hills, he flew away without touching the calf.

Jan followed the bird in her truck, tracking his radio signal to a roost site on nearby Brush Mountain. She wore jeans and a bulky light-blue goosedown jacket to ward off the cool air settling into the canyons. A Mickey Mouse hat covered her gray-flecked hair. She had purchased the wool hat after her son's San Marcos High basketball team defeated a crosstown rival that had derided them by calling their school Mickey Marcos High. Winning the game turned the name into a source of pride, and the hat became her talisman.

Jan had first encountered AC9 in 1980, when he was still a downy young chick in his nest, and over the years she had watched him mature into an adult bird. By 1987 a mere twenty-seven California condors were left in the world, and all but this one lived in captivity. The recovery effort Jan worked for represented the last hope for saving the species from extinction, and AC9 was crucial to their success.

The fading late-afternoon light forced Jan to make a critical decision. Years later, when she told me the story, that moment was still a vivid memory. Having observed condors for more than a dozen years, she could predict what would happen next. AC9 had seen the carcass, but hadn't eaten yet. He would surely come back the next day. Jan considered her next move. Should she notify her fellow condor biologists to set a trap for AC9 in the morning? Or should she simply turn her truck homeward, leaving the last wild condor his freedom? She realized that not a single soul in the world knew about this except her. She could call in the team to capture AC9. But if she didn't make that call, no one would ever know.

The hands of Jan's watch crept toward 6 P.M. Doing nothing was a decision by default—she needed to take charge, to make up her mind. Had any other human ever confronted such a quandary, she wondered: knowingly capturing the last wild member of a species? Despite the work of all the science panels and government agencies, tonight, this decision was hers alone. Earlier in the day she'd listened as the call of a red-tailed hawk echoed down a nearby canyon; she knew her call would reverberate even louder and longer, quite probably through the rest of her life. She thought again: *This recovery effort is the last hope.*

She pulled her Mickey Mouse hat tighter on her head and drove to a small Union 76 gas station to phone Pete Bloom. Bloom, a condor trapper for the National Audubon Society, listened to Jan and told her he would make some calls. The next day was Easter Sunday, and Jan knew that the odds of assembling the required team members were dicey. But Bloom's calls got through, and a half dozen scientists arrived at the site before dawn.

With mixed emotions, Bloom worked in the darkness with the other biologists to prepare the trap site. Bloom had spent his life trapping raptors, but he knew that this morning's capture attempt would be different—and critical. He placed blasting caps and metal weights into four pipes buried in the ground. The weights were tied to a folded, sixty-square-foot net. When the blasting caps were detonated, the weights would shoot the net several feet into the air, arcing over the calf carcass and ensnaring the bird. Normally, Bloom test-fired the net to make sure that it was correctly aligned—he didn't want one of the flying metal weights to hit a condor. But this morning, with AC9 roosting nearby, he didn't dare risk a test firing. He checked the setup a final time, and then hid himself in a one-person underground blind to begin the wait. The rest of the team concealed themselves a few hundred yards away. Once Bloom pushed the red detonator button, he would race to the net and restrain AC9 until the rest of the team arrived to help.

Easter morning dawned clear, cool, and breezy. Jan rose at 5 A.M. and drove back toward the roosting spot, passing alfalfa fields covered with veneers of ice from irrigation sprinklers. At 8:47 Jan's radio receiver came to life. *Click, click, click*: AC9 was stirring. Around 9:30 he headed toward the trap site, with Jan following. At 9:50 he landed fifteen yards east of the carcass. A few ravens picked at the calf. Jan observed through her spotting scope as AC9 danced toward the bait, and then edged back. Knowing what was about to happen renewed her doubts. She wanted to send the bird a message: *Get out of there.*

AC9 inched closer to the calf and lowered his head to feed. Pete Bloom detonated the explosives, and the net shot up from the ground and dropped over AC9. Bloom raced to the net, and within minutes the team had untangled AC9 and placed the bird in a portable pet carrier called a sky kennel. Jan's field notes from that morning are cryptic: *10:10, cannon fired. AC9 caught. The end.* The condor recovery program had crossed the Rubicon.

Jan wiped her eyes and exchanged an emotional hug with Pete Bloom. Like Jan, Bloom felt the magnitude of the moment. It was both the high point and the low point of his life. He had been hired to capture California condors, but trapping the last one filled him with both elation in successfully completing his job and great sadness at what it meant.

Jan thought about how the firing of the cannon net changed her world. With AC9 now a captive, she mourned the loss of her career as a condor biologist. Her days of following the wild birds ended that morning with a puff of smoke and the odor of cordite. Later in the day, she drove the mountain roads back to the program's headquarters at the Condor Research Center in Ventura. After all the years she had spent working with the recovery team in this untamed backcountry, the route to Ventura became a road of memories. She passed Pine Mountain and her eyes automatically went to the sky. No condors. She proceded on through the Los Padres National Forest. No condors. She continued into Ventura County. The horizon remained empty. For Jan, it was as if the sky had become devoid of all birds. Something elemental was missing.

Jan arrived at the Condor Research Center to find the staff besieged with calls from the media. Her boss asked if she would help field questions about AC9's capture. She had an instant, visceral reaction: *I can't do that today.* In an uncharacteristic move that surprised her even as she spoke the word, Jan said, "No." That afternoon, she simply couldn't talk rationally about the capture. Instead, she sat in her office and let the emotions of the day wash over her. For the first time in tens of thousands of years, not a single California condor flew over North America. The magnificent titan of the air that some Native Americans called Thunderbird had vanished from the sky.

Jan made herself a promise: *One day AC9 will again fly free.* But the promise filled her with trepidation, partly because the salvation of the condor now rested in other hands. Whether the U.S. government's condor recovery program could achieve its ambitious goal of saving America's largest bird was uncertain, especially when so much about the species remained a mystery. In fact, on that Easter Sunday in 1987, as the recovery team transported AC9 to the San Diego Zoo's Wild Animal Park, they had yet to breed a single condor in captivity.

In the years preceding AC9's birth, biologists had grown increasing alarmed at the declining number of California condors. A 1978 study prepared for the U.S. Forest Service presented a gloomy forecast of the bird's prospects. Another report, issued the same year by a panel of scientists selected by the American Ornithologists' Union and the National Audubon Society, reached similar conclusions. Something had to change—and quickly—or the only condors left would be museum specimens.

The National Audubon Society used their political clout to press for a more intensive government-sponsored condor program. At the same time, they offered to become a partner in the new project and to partially fund it. Their efforts succeeded. In 1979, under the auspices of the U.S. Fish & Wildlife Service and the National Audubon Society, a revamped condor program was established. Data collection and close field observations formed the core of the new effort. That meant equipping some of the birds with radio transmitters. Not only would the tiny transmitters allow biologists to track the birds, but radiotelemetry could help find the bodies of birds that died so it might be determined what had killed them. The new approach also placed a high priority on establishing a captive-breeding program. With so few birds left, starting a zoo-based population offered a crucial safety net for the species.

The U.S. Fish & Wildlife Service named one of its biologists, Noel Snyder, to lead their part of the effort. Yet when Snyder took his new position early in 1980, he had virtually no experience with condors; he had only seen the bird once, on a trip to California ten years earlier. An intense but affable man with thinning hair and a salt-and-pepper beard, Snyder possessed a keen intellect, a prodigious work ethic, and an impressive resume. He held a Ph.D. in evolutionary biology from Cornell University and had worked to save both an endangered parrot species and the Everglade kite.

Prior to his selection, Snyder had been one of the biologists asked to review the new recommendations for saving the condor. The data-based approach impressed him. From his experience helping

other birds hovering on the edge of extinction, Snyder believed scientists needed to plan their interventions based on solid evidence of
the factors behind a species' decline. And as strange as it may seem,
no one at the time knew for certain what was causing the condor's
troubles.

The new "activist program" Snyder sought to implement flew
in the face of traditional condor conservation methods. In many
quarters, the mere mention of radio transmitters—much less captive breeding—was taboo. Condor traditionalists held that the bird
needed only to be left alone and given enough habitat for its numbers to recover. A cadre of influential scientists and conservationists favored this approach, basing their arguments on a firm
foundation: the work of Carl Koford, the first scientist to make a
detailed study of the California condor. Koford's published work,
based upon research conducted in the late 1930s and 1940s, portrayed the condor as an extremely sensitive bird. According to Koford and his followers, trapping and radio-tagging condors would
cause the remaining birds grave harm. Some respected environmental organizations also adopted the "let-them-live-free" banner.
In the end, who was one to believe: Koford, a respected scientist
who had written the defining work on the species, or a bunch of
government outsiders who wanted to invade nests, strap radios on
some birds, and send others to live in zoos?

Snyder recognized the obstacles he faced in trying to save the
condor, but as he and his wife headed west to begin working on the
new project, he had no idea of the political maelstrom that awaited
him. It wouldn't be many months before the politics of saving the
bird became more challenging than the science.

O

As soon as Snyder arrived in California in 1980, he began explor-
ing condor country. And remarkably, on his second day in the field,
he hit pay dirt. John Borneman, the National Audubon Society
condor warden, took Snyder and his wife, Helen, to a mountaintop

near Interstate 5 to look at old nest sites. Helen noticed two tiny black specks flying in the distant sky.

"Condors," she said. They watched the birds swoop across a sandstone escarpment and disappear into the cliff face.

Snyder turned to Borneman. "Any nesting going on in that area?"

Borneman said it was only known as a roosting area.

"But it's a pair," Snyder said.

They found the nest the following day. The birds at this new site were AC9's parents-to-be. Since there was only one other condor nest known to exist that year, the find held enormous significance. Jan Hamber could only shake her head and marvel at Snyder's magic touch. She had been trekking through the back-country for months looking unsuccessfully for condor nests, yet this newcomer had found one in only two days. She hoped that he understood how much effort she had expended and how difficult nests were to find.

AC9's parents were using a nest cave partway up a sandstone cliff. Two entrances to the cave—each roughly four feet in diameter—were positioned just a few feet apart. Above these entrances, a broad diagonal vein of white rock slashed across the reddish cliffs that soared to the sky. The site offered easy viewing through a spotting scope from across the steep canyon. From the best vantage point about a third of a mile away, team members could look slightly down and directly into the twin entrances of the cave. The two openings peered from the cliffs like the eyes of a Tiki god.

Snyder enlisted a coterie of other recovery team members and volunteers to keep constant watch on AC9's nest site. The team established a comfortable observation post across the canyon, spreading a tarp on the ground and setting up some folding aluminum chairs. They strung another tarp overhead to protect them from the sun and rain. Spotting scopes were trained on the twin cave entrances throughout the daylight hours, and observers kept careful field notes on all of the condors' activities. They called the parent condors the CC pair. Thus, the female became CCF and the male CCM.

Around the third week of March 1980, CCF began spending more time within the cave's sheltering walls. She worked at smoothing and contouring the sandy floor with her bill, sometimes gathering a stone or twig in her beak and flinging it over her shoulder. The ancient birthing rite that had sustained her species for more than forty thousand years was about to begin. Although CCF had no way of knowing it, she was about to give birth to one of the most important birds in the history of *Gymnogyps californianus*.

One chilly day, a series of mild contractions swept CCF's body. Stronger tremors followed. The contractions gained in intensity, pulsating through her every ten to fifteen seconds. She stood over the sandy spot in the cave that she had prepared. She lifted and spread her tail feathers. A powerful tremor shuddered through her body. Her back arched, her neck stiffened, and her eyes narrowed. She gave a hoarse squeal. A four-inch-long egg shot out of her cloaca and landed with a thud on the sand.

For a minute CCF did not move. She then turned and touched the egg gently with her bill, a benediction to new life. In the cave's half-light, the shell shined the palest of blues. For ten minutes, CCF examined her egg, rolling and nuzzling the wet, warm orb. When she was ready, she tucked it on top of her feet and settled over it with her breast.

At the time AC9's egg was laid, Jan had responsibility for monitoring the only other known condor nest, which was located in Santa Barbara County. But the visibility into the nest site wasn't nearly as good as the one monitored by Snyder—on top of which, Jan had never seen a condor egg. So as soon as CCF laid her egg, Jan made time to visit Snyder's observation post.

As Jan hiked into the site, she could hear the cries of a nesting pair of prairie falcons calling from the cliff above the condors' nest cave. Jan peered through a Questar telescope and focused the image. She thought about how even an ordinary egg—at once both delicate and strong—embodies perfection and contains the promise of carrying the past into the future. The exquisite rarity of a condor egg amplified Jan's anticipation. In the cave's dim light, the parent bird rose up, revealing the egg. More than thirty years later, Jan still remembers that moment with wonderment. There, on the cave's dirt floor, the egg glowed like a giant jewel.

The CC pair spent the next two months incubating and caring for their egg. The birds worked in shifts; while one attended the nest, the other took to the sky to forage for food. Both birds remained alert for predators such as ravens, who liked nothing better than to drive their heavy bills into condor eggs and then eat the contents. Snyder's team caught glimpses of the egg when the sitting adult condor turned it or took a break to stretch its wings at the cave entrance. The birds moved the egg often, rolling it with their bills and sometimes even kicking it with their feet. When the pair made an incubating exchange, they left the nest site and sometimes spent a few minutes together weaving a languid sky dance above the canyon.

Despite the remoteness of the site, human activity was never far away. The reports of hunting rifles echoed up the canyon. Sonic booms rattled the cliffs. Once, a helicopter swooped down the canyon and thundered directly overhead. There were also natural elements to contend with. The observers endured heat and cold and poison oak and the buzz of rattlesnakes. As spring moved toward summer, the canyon became an oven, with temperatures often reaching well above 100°F. Snyder spent long days observing the birds. The heat caused him to dehydrate, and he endured several excruciating bouts of kidney stones.

Condors incubate their eggs for just under two months, so by early May the team started paying close attention for signs of hatching. At midmorning on May 11, Helen Snyder, the observer that day, noticed that the incubating bird seemed agitated. The bird kept getting up, rolling the egg, and moving dirt about in the nest. Perhaps, Helen wondered, the adult bird could hear the chick moving inside the egg. In the late afternoon she bent over the telescope and finally saw what they had all been waiting for: a raised area on the egg's shell the size of a fingernail. "Pipping" had begun. It was a critical time for the emerging bird: the hatching of a condor often takes as long as two or three days, and some chicks perish from exhaustion while fighting their way out of the giant egg.

In the late afternoon, Noel Snyder arrived to relieve his wife. He saw an hourglass-shaped hole in the egg. Every now and then the chick's egg tooth—a hooked appendage on its tiny beak designed for breaking through the shell—popped in and out of sight as the chick worked to free himself.

To his delight, early the next morning Snyder could see that the chick had managed to poke an inch-wide hole in the shell. CCF helped out by using her great beak, designed for tearing apart dead animals, to gently break off fragments of the shell and assist her tiny chick make its entrance into the world. The sun rose, heating the canyon air, and the view through the telescope lost its focus, dissolving into a shimmering Impressionistic tableau. Through the blur, CCF could be seen attending the egg: a good sign.

On the third day, Snyder's team watched the hole in the egg grow larger and caught the first glimpses of the chick's head. But its progress seemed agonizingly slow, and when the sun set, it had not yet emerged. The fate of the tiny chick, upon whom hope for the species might rest, hung in the balance. If the bird could not break out of the egg in the next few hours, it would die.

Sometime during the night of May 13, out of sight of human eyes, CCF's struggling chick broke free of its eggshell and stepped into a darkened world. CCF cuddled her newborn son close for warmth, and for these two condors, the world was as it had always been. The night air smelled of cool sandstone mixed with the astringent odor of ammonia from the whitewash of excrement trailing down the rocky escarpment. Up the canyon, a fox barked. It was a scene that had been repeated for thousands of years. Except that now, CCF's chick was one of fewer than three dozen California condors remaining in the world.

The next morning the canyon filled with the kind of silence that sinks into your bones. A scattering of stars faded with the coming sunrise. The observation team set up the telescope at first light and noticed a large piece of eggshell sitting at the cave entrance. Less than an hour later, CCF stood up and revealed her chick: a not-yet-dry yellow ball of fluff snuggling next to his mother. It looked so normal that it seemed possible for a moment to imagine that the future of these ancient birds was as solid as the layers of compressed time frozen in the cliff's sedimentary rocks.

The observers watched the rising sun color the sandstone cliff in hues of red and magenta. The young chick wobbled on unsteady legs in the recesses of the cave, sometimes falling on his face or side. The adult birds fed AC9 several times during the morning and afternoon, and by evening his stability improved. He had survived his first day of life.

AC9's parents would need to care for the chick for nearly a year before he would achieve full independence. Many perils fill this vulnerable time for any young condor, but the circumstances of AC9's birth raised the stakes to an extraordinary level. While this tiny, one-day-old chick couldn't know what awaited him in the weeks ahead, he would soon learn that danger would be his relentless companion.

2

Naked Vulture

ON A SUMMER morning in 2005 I arrive at the Santa Barbara Museum of Natural History. I'm here to visit the museum's Condor Archives, one of the nation's largest repositories of condor knowledge. I drive past the oak and eucalyptus trees that surround the museum's elegant Mediterranean-style buildings set in the shadow of the towering Santa Ynez Mountains. I continue past the main building and park in front of a two-story Victorian house converted for museum use. My destination is a first-floor office that holds the archives.

This treasure trove of information is managed by Jan Hamber.

In 1959, Jan, her husband, and their young family arrived in Santa Barbara to start a new life. She had just received her biology degree from Cornell University and was determined to pursue her girlhood dream of being a field naturalist. Soon after her move west, she dropped her son off for his first day of kindergarten, drove to the Santa Barbara Museum of Natural History, and asked how she could help out. They put Jan to work straightway. Nearly a half-century later, she's still there.

By the mid-1970s, the museum had Jan hiking Santa Barbara's backcountry and monitoring a pair of nesting condors. When Noel Snyder arrived there in 1980 to begin the new condor recovery project, Jan offered to help. Wisely, Snyder made good use of her already considerable knowledge. In the years that followed, her contribution to the condor effort earned her the nickname, "The Queen Mother of the Recovery Program."

When I walk into the archives' office, I find Jan at her computer muttering about the glut of spam. "I can't believe people think I'd want to *buy* all this junk," she says. Jan punctuates her sentences with quick hand movements and a ready smile. In her jeans and Condor Recovery Team T-shirt, she looks much as she did in recovery program pictures from twenty-five years ago.

Jan is organized and precise about details, yet she is surrounded by scattered stacks of papers and books. Managing the archives is a big job for one person—it's hard to stay caught up.

Jan and I have talked before, but today I've arranged for us to spend a longer time together. I settle into a chair and look around. Condor pictures cover the walls, and a menagerie of toy condors is scattered about the room. But what really grabs my attention are nine four-drawer filing cabinets and several floor-to-ceiling bookcases jammed with field notes, books, and records from years of research. For someone interested in condors, this is nirvana.

My plan is to spend the morning; I end up staying two days.

○

Later in the day, Jan takes me into one of the museum's halls, where a huge, free-standing, glass-enclosed display dominates the room. Inside the exhibit is a preserved condor flying over the Santa Barbara backcountry. The display gives you the dramatic perspective of looking at the bird at eye level. Underneath the condor lies a panoramic relief map that stretches dozens of miles from the Sierra Madre Mountains to the Channel Islands in the distance. It's cleverly scaled to make the bird appear a mile or more up in the sky.

As if we're looking out the window of an airplane, Jan points out various rivers and valleys where she spent years watching condors. A young boy and his mother approach the exhibit, and Jan bends over to help the child with the display's earphones. I study the scene. I've watched a lot of condors, but never from the angle of looking straight at a bird in flight from just a few feet away. The display's perspective makes it seem as if you're flying alongside the bird. You can almost hear the wind, feel a rush of vertigo. The swirl of colors on the head—orange, pink, black, brown—is rendered just right, and the wings spread beyond wide. The bird angles through the sky, its left wing raised to reveal the broad white triangle on the underside. It's not just the size but the bulk of the broad-backed bird that grabs my eye. Condors typically weigh a hefty twenty to twenty-two pounds, although I've seen released birds that topped the scales at twenty-five pounds. I want to turn to Jan and say, "It's huge!" but I'm afraid it'll sound silly.

I'm also wondering if people realize the significance of this bird that biologists called AC3. How many visitors know that this was the last of the wild condors to die? The mother and son who are beside us have no idea that Jan spent years watching this very bird in the wild. Or that AC3 figured in two tragic episodes that Jan pinpoints as the lowest points in her career. Or that AC3's long and horrible death forever changed the recovery program. But I'm getting ahead of my story.

Lift your arms so they are parallel to the ground. Double that distance. That's roughly the wingspan of a condor in flight. Imagine that you're AC3, soaring on giant wings that allow you to slip gravity's bounds. You catch a rising column of air and ride it like an elevator a mile into the sky. As you float in a dreamy glide over the landscape, the ridges and canyons below form a mosaic of rock and chaparral. Want to change direction? Simply turn your tail or adjust a few of your two-foot-long primaries—the feathers that spread from the ends of your wings like fingers. You ride the thermals for as much as one hundred and fifty miles in a day, sailing on top of the world.

Jan interrupts my musings. "Let's take a look in the vertebrate zoology labs." As we leave the hall, I glance back at the display. *Geez, that's a big bird.*

○

Condor. The name belongs to the two largest and most majestic vultures of the Americas: the California condor and the Andean condor. The two birds are approximately the same size and share many characteristics, including their name.

"Condor" comes from the Quechua word *cuntur*. Quechua, the language of the Incas, is still used today by millions of people in South America. The moniker "California condor" only came into widespread use in the twentieth century. Early European settlers called the great bird the California vulture or the royal vulture. The Spanish used several variants of *buitre*, their word for vulture. And Native American cultures had dozens of different names for the condor. Some of these names were used for condor chicks hatched at the beginning of the captive-breeding program.

The condor's scientific name, *Gymnogyps californianus*, literally means "naked vulture of California." Of course, the bird itself isn't naked—only its head and neck lack feathers. The reference to California is also a bit of a misnomer. It's true that the bird's range in recent times has been limited largely to that state, but two or three hundred years ago, the bird roamed the full length of the West, from Baja California to Washington State.

Both the California and Andean condors are members of the family Cathartidae (which means "cleansers"), more commonly known as the New World vultures. Unlike some of the other birds in this family, male and female California condors look identical: only a blood test will reveal their gender. In addition to condors, five other vulture species belong to the New World vultures of the Americas, including the ubiquitous turkey vulture. Although this group bears a superficial resemblance to the Old World vultures—another family related to eagles and hawks—most ornithologists think that the New World vultures are actually more closely linked to storks.

Several characteristics distinguish New World vultures: they have naked heads, their feet have evolved for walking instead of carrying prey, they don't build traditional nests, and they have very limited vocalization capabilities. In addition, these carrion eaters cool themselves by excreting waste on their legs: the drying excreta lower the temperature of their circulating blood.

Vultures have adopted a unique survival strategy—in order for them to eat, another creature must die. These birds live a life in which accidents, disease, other predators, and good luck determine their next meal. In contrast, most meat-eating mammals will both scavenge *and* hunt for food. Among the roughly ten thousand bird species on the planet, only a tiny group—twenty-two worldwide—pin their livelihood on scavenging. Condors live a life where they must be observant—and ever so patient. And smart.

According to Noel Snyder, the condor's mental acumen evolved from having to operate in a complex environment that puts a premium on intelligence. Not only are condors very social with one another, but they also have to deal with many other species at a kill site. The situations there are often not repeatable and can be life threatening. A condor's existence is not simple, and a bird courts disaster if it makes a mistake with a golden eagle or a mountain lion that may be lurking around a carcass. These predators offer no second chance to learn from an error. Many biologists compare the condor's intelligence to that of primates. Although it can't be proved—the data isn't there yet—it's a reasonable hypothesis that condors are brilliant. In any event, one thing is certain: a condor is one of the smartest birds on the planet.

○

Jan wants to show me some specimens in the museum's private vertebrate zoology labs. This high-ceilinged area doubles as a museum work space: cement floor, florescent lights, and wood-and-metal museum cases fill the maze of rooms. Specimens in various states of construction cover work tables. We're looking for Cathartidae.

"Here it is," Jan says. She pulls out a shoulder-high wooden tray filled with condor artifacts. The smell of mothballs jolts me backward. Jan removes several black flight feathers nearly as long as my arm. I feel their stiffness and strength. Next I pick up a wing bone that is longer than my forearm and as light as the feathers. A tiny window cut into the bone allows me to see its thin walls and hollow insides.

"Look at the skull." Jan puts the lower mandible in place for the full effect. I touch the hooked beak.

"That's sharp!"

Jan's eyes twinkle. "The better to eat you with, my dear."

Condor bodies are designed to make the most of consuming a carcass. The hooked bill tears through flesh, and the long neck allows it to work its way into a dead body. The feather-free head and neck make it easier to stay clean. While condors prefer fresh carcasses, they will consume meat that's—shall we say—past its prime. To do this, they have evolved a powerful resistance to bacterial toxins such as botulism so that they can eat with impunity. What the skull doesn't show is the impressive capacity for learning that helps the condor survive in a hostile world.

As Jan takes me to look at a condor egg—it's in the oology department—we talk about the condor's even larger ancestors. Remains of the *Teratornis merriami*, a condorlike bird that had a twelve-foot wingspan, have been found at the La Brea Tar Pits in Los Angeles. This bird may well have been seen by early humans. *Teratornis incredibilis*, with an estimated wingspan of seventeen feet, was another even larger condor ancestor that also flew over North America. And to put things in perspective, *Argentavis magnificens*, an extinct behemoth from Argentina, holds the record for the largest flying bird of all time, with a wingspan of twenty-three feet and weighing in at more than 160 pounds. If one of those creatures ever visits your campground, give it what it wants.

The museum has one condor egg, which is stored in a clear plastic case. In order to remove the egg's contents, someone drilled a one-eighth-inch hole into the shell. An inscription inked in neat black letters beside the hole tells me the egg is from 1936. The white shell has a few brownish spots and a grayish tinge that may have come from age. Jan describes for me the delicate green or light-blue hues of a newly laid egg. Early in the twentieth century, one condor egg could be worth hundreds of dollars to collectors. In fact, in order to turn a quick profit, unscrupulous egg collectors sometimes substituted swan eggs for condor eggs.

Condors often keep the same mate for many years, and since the birds can live 50 or 60 years, their relationships are long-term and complex. Parent condors lay just a single egg, so baby chicks are always only children. The parents incubate the egg for just under two months, but that's only the beginning of their task. Raising a condor chick takes a long time — often close to a year. Condor parents will skip egg laying the following year if their chick has not yet fully fledged.

I carefully place the condor egg back in the tray. This condor chick never had a chance. Egg collecting was just one more way that humans led the species to the edge of extinction.

○

As my fascination with the giant birds grew, and the number of articles I read about the species ran into the hundreds, I noticed a pattern emerging in how condors were portrayed. Writers unfamiliar with the bird often described it as a relic, a throwback, an evolutionary misfit, a creature whose time had passed, an overly sensitive holdover from the Pleistocene era. It makes me wince to hear the condor described as a senescent species. Not only is it wrong, but it carries the implication that this marvelous and well-adapted creature has no place in the modern world. These erroneous assertions about the condor have gone on for decades. As early as 1942, biologist Loye Miller described the condor this way: "Is not the California Condor a senile species that is far past its prime?"

Granted, the condor species is at least forty thousand years old. But other birds are much older. Loons and grebes, for example, trace their origins back *millions* of years. And let's not forget that our own ancestors were also there in the Pleistocene. In fact, most species alive today have an ancestry that dates back at least as far as that era. There are simply no data anywhere to show that the condor is anything but a tough, scrappy, well-adapted survivor. Like so many living things these days, the condor's problems stem directly from the actions of one species: *Homo sapiens*.

The condor's human troubles began eleven thousand years ago at a time when dozens of large mammal species roamed North America's immense wilderness: woolly mammoths, camels, sloths, giant bears. The condor feasted on the carcasses of these great creatures. The birds ranged across vast sections of the continent, and fossil remains of condors have been found throughout the West, in Florida, and even in New York.

The continent's landscape began to change when the first groups of *Homo sapiens* spread across North America. Despite this new species' lack of speed and muscle power, it proved a formidable predator. These early humans were expert hunters, able to bring down animals as huge as a six-ton mastodon. The arrival of humans coincided with a mass extinction of more than fifty large mammal species. We may never be able to prove it, but it seems more than a coincidence that as soon as humans arrived, so many large animals disappeared. We certainly see similar patterns repeated in different areas around the world where the arrival of early humans heralded the end of the big animals. In North America, the death of so many species is known as the Pleistocene overkill. The loss of much of the Pleistocene megafauna drastically reduced the condor's food supply.

One would think that the birds might have fed on the great herds of bison that blanketed the prairies, but apparently the American buffalo's migration patterns took them too far from areas suitable for condor nest sites to make the bison a reliable food source. In time, the bird's range shrank to the continent's west coast. There, in the canyons and coastal ranges of the American West, the condor fed on tule elk, mule deer, beached whales, and even spawning salmon. In this way, it sustained itself nicely for the next several thousand years.

○

Few wild chicks of any species have been observed as closely as AC9. The field notes from the first months of his life — recorded by observers who watched him through spotting scopes from an observation post across the canyon — fill hundreds of pages. Jan helps me find the three bulging notebooks on AC9, and we lug them into a nearby conference room.

I begin reading. The notes paint a detailed picture of every moment from that spring of 1980, when . . . it isn't long before I, too, feel as if I am watching the birds from that observation post.

○

For the first couple of weeks of AC9's life, one of his parents, CCF or CCM, stayed with him constantly, cuddling close to provide warmth and protection. While one of the parents brooded the chick, the other searched for food. The nest site became a contrast of colors: the bodies of the adult birds forming a black background for AC9's fluffy white down.

AC9 spent the days sleeping and resting near one of his parents. Sometimes the parent bird linked necks with AC9, rubbing and preening his body; in turn, AC9 would nuzzle the adult. But the chick became most animated when one of the adults returned from a foraging trip. AC9 knew that the arrival of a parent meant food, and he already had a condor-sized appetite. When one his parents appeared, AC9 opened his bill wide and beat his tiny wings with furious insistence.

Accustomed to her chick's hunger, CCF took her time when she returned to the cave. First she rested from her flight. Sometimes she stroked AC9's tiny body with her beak and let him beg. AC9 would flap his wings harder and make soft hissing sounds. When his wing beats became too frantic, CCF nipped at him. Finally she opened her beak and allowed AC9 to plunge his head into her throat. AC9 greedily gobbled up his meal. Often the feedings lasted only twenty or thirty seconds. When CCF grew tired of feeding her chick, she placed her foot on AC9's neck and pushed him away. Such is condor love.

During daylight hours, unless AC9 was hidden in the recesses of the cave, observers noted his every movement. What we know less about are his parents. Their activities at the nest site were, as a matter of course, also meticulously documented. But once they winged their way over the horizon to search for food, we can only guess at what happened.

Jan told me that back in the days before birds were equipped with radio transmitters, researchers who wanted to learn where condors nested and foraged enlisted her help.

"How shall I discover where they go?" she asked.

"Just watch when the birds fly out of sight," came the answer. "Then, go to that spot. When the birds fly by the next time, follow them again. Do that until you find where they go."

I laughed at the impossibility of moving about in a land of knife-edged ridges and impenetrable chaparral.

Jan smiled. "Plus, condors don't take the same route each time."

So we can only speculate where AC9's parents went during their foraging expeditions and what they did once they arrived at their destination. In-depth research over the past twenty-five years, however, has given us a very accurate picture of how condors fly, look for food, and navigate a kill site. Using this research, we can piece together what a typical foraging trip might have been like in the days after AC9's birth:

On a morning in May, CCF preened herself at the cave entrance and stretched her wings to dry the dew that collected in her feathers overnight. Her mate had returned the evening before with a bulging crop, and it now fell to her to search for food. She stretched her wings one last time and launched into the air.

CCF didn't fly more than a few yards before a prairie falcon dove at her and forced her to land on a boulder below the nest. A pair of prairie falcons had set up house-keeping on the cliff above the condors, and in order to get in and out of their nest, the parent birds often had to run this annoying gauntlet of screams and talons.

CCF shook herself, refolded her wings, and walked back to the cave to try again. This time she succeeded in evading the falcon and wheeled into the sky. She soared down the canyon and turned south, stopping at the body of a deer killed by a mountain lion just a few miles away. She knew the site, having scavenged there three days ago. Today she found a golden eagle picking at the carcass. Like most condors, CCF usually deferred to golden eagles at a kill site, and anyway, not much remained of the deer.

Now CCF flew inland toward more open country. She soared high over ripening orchards and plowed fields, past highways and houses. After more than an hour, her keen eyes spotted several turkey vultures circling in the distance. She headed their way. Condors often rely on other birds to find their carcasses for them, and today the turkey vultures had found a jackpot: a freshly killed pig sprawled on a rock outcropping on a grassy hill.

Patience held the key to navigating the often-complicated situation at a kill site. CCF circled overhead and surveyed the scene with care. Was the pig really dead, or perhaps simply resting? Were there other predators lurking nearby waiting to pounce? An ugly bullet wound had torn open the pig's flank. He lay on a plateau near the edge of a small cliff, still as death. Circling wider, she observed where the pig had dragged himself up the rocky hill, leaving splashes of blood. He'd made it to the cliff's edge before collapsing. Half a dozen vultures, along with a couple of ravens, were already on the ground near the pig. One bold raven hopped onto the pig's head—and the pig lurched to his feet. The bird screamed. Blinded by pain, the pig lost his balance and rolled over the cliff. His body smashed into a boulder twenty feet below.

CCF waited on a nearby snag while the other birds returned to the now very dead pig. She waited until several turkey vultures were standing on the pig's body. She waited until the ravens pecked out the eyes. Finally, like a queen, CCF dropped slowly to the ground and strode forward to take her place at the carcass. The other birds moved aside to let CCF feed. Flies buzzed, and the air quivered with heat radiating from the cliff's pale rocks. If the pig had not fallen over the small cliff, CCF probably would have thrust her bare head into the carcass at the place where the bullet had ripped open the pig's tough hide. But the fall onto the boulder broke the pig open in a half dozen places. CCF used her sharp beak to tear chunks of meat from the pig's shoulder. It was lucky she didn't feed at the wound site, for a great and unknown danger would have awaited her there.

Shuffling about on the ground, CCF was—like all condors—an ungainly bird. She waddled around the pig, her black, shroud-like body aptly reminiscent of death. Her salmon-colored head and neck—bereft of feathers— resembled a vacuum-cleaner hose. The incongruous ruff at the base of her neck looked like an old lady's fur coat.

CCF filled her crop in just a few minutes. Tearing at the carcass in the midday sun made for hot work; to cool off, she lifted her tail and sprayed her legs with excreta. Finally, having eaten her fill, CCF walked to a nearby slope. To launch herself skyward, she ran downhill with a clumsy, hopping motion, lumbering more than thirty feet before she propelled herself upward. As she rose into the air, she left her awkward earthbound movements behind and transformed herself into a streamlined flying machine able to soar for hours. On her journey back to the nest site, CCF flapped her wings only once.

○

Worry tempered the joy that Snyder and other team members felt in watching AC9 develop. At the time of AC9's birth in 1980, fewer than three dozen California condors remained in the world, and basic questions about the condor's biology still remained unanswered. Could these condors be successfully bred in captivity? Why was the bird is such desperate trouble, and what was causing its decline? No one knew. The recovery team didn't even know exactly how many condors were left in the wild. One fact was certain: the bird's numbers were plummeting toward extinction.

Meanwhile, AC9 and his parents spent their days blissfully unaware of their species' troubles. The weeks passed, and AC9 grew a thick coat of dark gray down. Within a month, he could maintain his body temperature well enough that he no longer needed the cuddling warmth of his parents during the day. His parents left him alone at the nest site for many of the daylight hours while they searched for food to satisfy his ever-growing appetite. One of them always returned at night.

One evening AC9 waited for the familiar rustle of wings and the scrape of claws on rock. The nest grew darker and a yellow moon filled the sky. He shuffled around the nest cave and beat his stubby wings a few times. It would still be months before he could fly. The night air pulsed with crickets. With no sign of his parents, AC9 huddled against the cold stone in the back of the cave and dozed fitfully. Down the canyon, a coyote howled. Sometime in the night a breeze came up; the stars glided through wind-driven clouds. After many hours, a wash of gray light colored the sky, and the sun finally turned the haze on the horizon to copper. Insects buzzed; AC9 beat his wings in hunger. He moved to the cave entrance and looked skyward.

His parents were nowhere in sight.

While AC9 huddled in the nest cave, he was unaware that across the canyon a human observer monitored his every move. When night had fallen, the recovery team member noted that both adult birds had not returned, but he described this development without alarm. Once a condor chick reaches a few weeks of age, it is not unusual for the parent birds to leave the nest for longer periods, roaming farther afield to find food for the growing chick.

At first light the next morning, the observer began his usual note taking, recording the air temperature, wind direction, and sky conditions, and noting the calls of the prairie falcons on the nest cliff. He chronicled AC9's every movement. If AC9 flapped his wings, the field notes tell how many flaps. If he preened his feathers, it describes which ones and for how long. At mid-morning, CCM flew in from the west and arced downward through the dive-bombing prairie falcons. AC9 greeted his father by beating his wings in frenzied anticipation. Within minutes of his parent's landing, AC9 was fed.

3

Searching for Gymnogyps Californianus

NOEL SNYDER WAS hard at work in his office at the Condor Research Center in Ventura. It was late in May 1980, and Snyder was preparing for a crucial meeting with the California Fish and Game Commission. He needed permits from this state commission before condor data collection could begin, and there were no guarantees that these would be forthcoming. Nothing is simple in the bureaucracy surrounding a recovery effort, and Snyder knew that at the commission's upcoming public meeting, he would face stiff opposition from conservationists who would argue that radio-tagging the birds and developing a captive-breeding program would lead to the species' demise. But Snyder was absolutely convinced that without intensive hands-on management, the only data left to collect would be the date of the last bird's death.

The new management plan had already garnered much attention. The *Los Angeles Times* weighed in with a supporting editorial, urging the commission to grant the permits: "More [condors] die than are born every year and, barring human intercession, it is only a question of time before they vanish." But powerful opponents were forceful and very public in their criticism of this last-ditch effort to save the bird. They did not believe the last ditch had been reached. David Brower, the articulate founder of the conservation group Friends of the Earth, wrote a letter to the U.S. Secretary of Interior, asserting: "The condor deserves better than to be pushed toward extinction by enthusiasts of technological fixes. The proposed plan threatens to destroy the species in a misguided effort to save it."

Joining Brower were California chapters of the Sierra Club. They claimed that the permits the recovery team sought would authorize far too much manipulation of the birds, and made it clear that the Sierra Club did not condone this kind of experimentation. Instead, they argued that a ban on shooting and pesticide use in condor areas would allow the bird to recover on its own. They also maintained that preserving the condor's habitat was an essential component of the species' survival in the wild. Readily admitting that their concerns extended beyond the bird itself, they worried that capturing condors might open the way to development. Quite simply, having condors flying around made it easier to protect a number of important wilderness areas.

For some, the condor became a symbolic link to an ancient past of unfettered space and slow time. The bird came to be seen as a mystical creature representing a simpler, more pristine existence. Some argued it was better to let the condor die a death with dignity than to suffer the manipulations of scientists. Environmentalist Kenneth Brower, son of David Brower, wrote, "If it is time for the condor to [become extinct], it should go unburdened with radio transmitters."

Another vocal critic, rancher and naturalist Eben McMillan, also argued that the condor should be left in the wild, even if it meant sacrificing the bird. The lessons learned in trying to save the condor in its natural setting, he said, could then be applied to other endangered species. An intensive management program would only taint the process.

For many, these arguments held an emotional appeal. What hubris to think that we can so easily understand the complexities of another species. Who are we to radio-tag birds, manipulate their breeding, and proclaim to know what they need to survive? Ironically, Noel Snyder was never a supporter of captive-breeding programs: he believed then—and still argues today—that it is better to try every other option first and to only use captive breeding as a last resort. But in 1980, when he looked at the condor's dire predicament, the choice seemed clear: begin captive breeding or lose the species.

To a casual observer, the two sides were not even talking about the same bird. Which was the real condor—the highly sensitive bird needing space and solitude, or the curious, resilient bird who would benefit from hands-on intervention? In many ways, the condor itself disappeared behind the smoke and fury of the arguments and became instead a mirror reflecting human bias.

Snyder would ask the commission for permits to capture and examine condors. He wanted to place radio transmitters on ten birds, and to trap one bird as a mate for a bird called Topa Topa, the sole condor being held in captivity. This request was politically expedient but hardly practical. With less than thirty birds remaining, the recovery team needed to launch an aggressive captive-breeding program immediately.

Keen public interest prompted the commission to consider the permit request at a special nighttime meeting in a Santa Barbara theater. On that evening, Snyder and the recovery team confronted the full fervency of their adversaries. Hundreds of people, many of them long-haired folks in jeans and plaid shirts, filled the seats. The atmosphere grew tense as audience members shouted and interrupted the proceedings. One man had to be forcibly removed. During the public testimony, a long line of people stood to speak. Many of them made emotional pleas to protect the great bird, expressing fears that government technocrats would use "mutilative biology" to turn condors into zoo-raised feathered pigs.

As the public testimony wound down, a statuesque man with a shock of white hair strode to the end of the speaker's line. Several times he let others go ahead of him so that he would be the last to address the meeting. When he stepped to the microphone, a hush settled over the theater. He introduced himself as David Brower, leader of Friends of the Earth. He gazed calmly at the commissioners on stage, and in slow, stentorian tones, implored them to leave the condor alone.

"The condor is not an electronic toy to play with, rough up, blindfold, manhandle, peer into, draw blood from, wire for sound, tinker with its great wings, double-clutch, or put on crutches or behind bars." Brower gestured toward the recovery team. "We understand, but regret and deplore, the over-curiosity of the biologists who would invade the privacy of the condor and thus imperil one of the most famous and spectacular of all the endangered species. Give the bird the chance to save itself as a wild condor, not as a feathered radio transmitter, an alien bird under house arrest or a museum basket case." He ended by threatening legal action if the commission approved the permits.

Brower's speech brought down the house. Even those who disagreed with him could not help being moved by his eloquence. Nevertheless, as the five-and-a-half-hour meeting drew to a close, the commission reluctantly approved a scaled-back version of the original request that disallowed even simple data collection tools such as blood sampling. The decision pleased no one. The anticapture people were furious at the commission's support for handling and manipulating condors. Had they not heard Brower's charismatic presentation and the defiance of so many in the audience? The recovery team was not happy either. They had permission to undertake a few modest first steps, hardly what they deemed necessary to save a bird so close to extinction.

Little did either side know that this was only a skirmish in a conflict that would last for years. In fact, it is hard to think of a recovery effort before or since that has generated as much public attention or provoked as much ill will as the fight over the condor. As writer Charles Bergman said, "No one who touched the condor project came away without wounds."

○

How was it that the opposing sides seemed to be talking about such different birds? To better understand why the hands-on management versus the let-them-live-free camps came to face off over the fate of the last birds, I knew I needed to look back on how the human view of the condor had changed over time. I was surprised at what I found.

My journey to find the real condor began at the Museum of Vertebrate Zoology at the University of California at Berkeley. I entered the museum's gallery area, a huge room filled with waist-high metal drawers holding thousands of animal specimens. Perched atop some of these cabinets are mounted birds: a bald eagle, a wandering albatross, and a California condor that was collected in 1901.

I came to the museum to look at condor study skins. Rather than mount each specimen—which is an expensive process and requires a lot of storage space—museums often keep what are known as study skins. They resemble real birds—sort of. The organs, soft tissue, and most of the bones are removed. The remaining skin is stuffed with filler material and sewn shut. Small puffs of cotton poke through the eye sockets.

The condor study skins were in the top four drawers of one of the cabinets. I opened the first shoulder-high drawer and found a surprise. *Andean condors,* I said to myself. I noted the crest on the head. *A male.* I also discovered two other birds in the drawer: king vultures. I then found seven California condor skins with information tags tied to their inch-long claws. These were old birds, and the tags—yellow and brittle with age—noted when the birds died and where they were collected.

I removed the first study skin and placed it on a cart. It felt stiff, its colors dull. I smelled a faint odor of naphthalene. The neck and head were rigid, and the bright orange had faded to dark gray. I then looked at the others. These skins bore little resemblance to the birds I knew, as if they were not condors but a different and distant species. I could not help thinking that if the condor becomes extinct, all that will be left for future generations will be these sad, lifeless study skins sitting in metal drawers. As I worked, I noticed how quiet the gallery was—like a morgue.

Most of the study skins were more than a century old. They were shot in the 1880s, a time when many naturalists regarded the California condor as a rare oddity and sought to collect specimens while the bird still existed. Although some naturalists were already predicting the bird's demise, procurement for museums continued. So did egg collecting. What is most astonishing is the peculiarly incurious attitude held toward the bird. Here was this amazing creature, yet early naturalists knew next to nothing of its habits or habitat. At the end of the nineteenth century, when these study skins were collected, if a person wanted to know about California condors, he or she would still find useful information in the journals of Lewis and Clark from the *beginning* of that century. That's how little attention was paid to North America's biggest bird during this time.

In the Lewis and Clark journals, one finds a cryptic note from the October 28, 1805, meteorology report: "First Vulture of the Columbia seen today." Two days after this sighting, Captain Lewis saw a second condor. He shot at it and missed. For more than three months, while the expedition explored the Columbia River mouth, Lewis and Clark noted repeated condor sightings. In November, they killed their first condor. Captain Clark made a thorough examination of the bird, recording the measurements of its neck, tail feathers, claws, and its nine-and-a-half-foot wingspan. In February, expedition members shot condors that they found feeding on a whale carcass. Captain Lewis wrote a lengthy and detailed description of one of the birds and included a lifelike drawing of its head.

The Lewis and Clark expedition team crossed two important thresholds: they made the first detailed scientific field observations of the bird, and they used guns to kill the condor. From that time on, rifles—as well as poisonous lead bullets consumed by condors when eating hunter-shot game—became major factors in the condor's vanishing numbers. In fairness, esteemed naturalists from that era such as John James Audubon and Ernest Thompson Seton commonly killed animals to collect specimens. These were the days before high-powered optics, and if you wanted to look at a creature, you used "shotgun science." It was also an era intoxicated by the possibility of endless expansion and everlasting natural resources. What did it matter to shoot a few animals?

Two more early condor landmarks merit our investigation. Just a few years before Lewis and Clark described their "Vulture of the Columbia," a Scotsman named Archibald Menzies first identified the condor as a species. Menzies, a surgeon with the Vancouver expedition that explored North America's west coast, collected a condor near Monterey, California, in 1792 and returned it to the British Museum. This bird became the "type specimen": the exemplar from which the description of a new species is made. From that time on, scientists recognized the condor as a species. Thus, a bird that had been soaring over the continent for tens of thousands of years now officially existed—which was, of course, of no consequence whatsoever to the bird itself. The California condor type specimen is now housed in the Natural History Museum in London, half a world away from its habitat.

The other landmark goes back nearly two centuries further, to the first written record of the condor. It is found in the diary of Antonio de la Ascension, a Carmelite friar who accompanied the 1602 Sebastian Vizcaino expedition on its exploration of the California coast. Ascension saw a group of condors feeding on a whale carcass and described the bird as looking like a large turkey. This is where the condor's early paper trail ends. But European explorers were not the only people familiar with the bird. The others, however, did not keep written records. And they had a decidedly different view of the condor.

> The drumbeat quickens and the singer's voice rises. The tribal elders seated on the ground of the ceremonial hut lean forward. All eyes are on the hut entrance as a giant bird darkens the doorway. The *Molokbe*—a condor impersonator—dances into the hut and moves slowly counterclockwise, ignoring those on the ground. The *Molokbe*

wears a condor skin stretched over his chest. Huge wings hang from his arms. Stripes of red paint circle his face, and feathers adorn his hair. The *Molokbe*'s dance quickens. He lifts his feather arms, preparing to carry the spirits of the dead to the next world on his giant wings.

For thousands of years Native Americans wove condors into the fabric of their lives, using the bird in ceremonies, artwork, and sacrifices. Many Native Americans thought that the condor—or, as some called it, the thunderbird—possessed supernatural powers. Thunderbird myths form one of the few cross-cultural elements among North American tribes ranging from the Plains Tribes to groups in the Pacific Northwest. Archeologists have unearthed condor bones in middens in Oregon that are at least nine thousand years old. And drawings and carvings of the condor are common among Pacific Northwest tribes. These thunderbird images often depict the condor as a benevolent helper that brings rain and creates thunder by flapping its mighty wings.

Although Native Americans revered the bird, they nonetheless took condors for domestication and used the bird in ritual sacrifice. One of the members of the 1769 Portola expedition that explored California for Spain described a group of Native Americans near the Monterey Bay who possessed both captive and stuffed condors. Impressed with the size of the bird, Portola named the area the Pajaro Valley—or Bird Valley.

Although Native Americans did have a negative effect on the condor population, it was not critically deleterious. European settlers, however, held a different philosophy. And they came carrying potent tools of steel and steam that allowed them to realize their world view.

Many European settlers did not care for or respect condors. While Native Americans saw the condor as a mythical, godlike creature, for many settlers, condors conjured up the macabre and evoked a primitive dread of death. The cultural roots that fostered this revulsion go deep. Vultures are an uncomfortable reminder that despite Western culture's attempts to bend nature to our will, we all die—and we are consumed. References in the Old Testament's Book of Leviticus caution readers to avoid the "detestable" vulture. Even Charles Darwin himself spoke of vultures as, "These disgusting birds, with their bald, scarlet heads, formed to revel in putridity." It is interesting that condors were—and sometimes still are—reviled for scavenging on the rotting remains of dead animals. I wonder how many people who feel this way have ever visited a slaughterhouse?

○

In 1607, five years after Friar Ascension saw his first condors in Monterey Bay, a wooden ship sailed into Chesapeake Bay and made landfall at Jamestown Island. Even though these first settlers faced a brutal life at Jamestown—in the first two years more than two-thirds of them died—the colony managed to sustain itself. Jamestown's survival led to the founding of more colonies that soon spread along the eastern seaboard.

The Jamestown settlers knew nothing of condors, yet they unwittingly initiated an epoch of change that had profound implications for wildlife across the continent. The condor's decline did not happen in isolation. A mere four hundred years ago, the first colonists found a land of staggering abundance only lightly touched by Native Americans. Vast hardwood forests abounded with deer and turkeys and other game. The rivers and seas brimmed with fish, otters, lobsters, beavers, and mink. Millions of bison foraged in herds so huge that they blackened the boundless oceans of prairie. Captain Lewis described his view from a river in South Dakota: "This scenery already rich, pleasing, and beautiful was still farther heightened by emmense herds of buffaloe, deer elk and antelopes which we saw in every direction feeding on the hills and plains. It seemed as if those seens of visionary inchantment would never have an end."

Yet in the blink of an eye in geologic time, these "seens of visionary inchantment" were swept away. The uncharted Terra Incognita,
as early cartographers referred to North America, became farmland
and factories and cities, all hungry for more resources. The trickle of
colonists turned into a flood that surged westward, first on foot and
horseback, then via steamboats and railroads. Along the way, the
settlers applied their tools, building the Cumberland Road, the Erie
Canal, and the transcontinental railroad.

It was this transformation—some would call it mutilation—of
the environment that had a far more profound effect than predation
from the pioneers' guns. The centuries-old forests were cut indis-
criminately, and the hardwood turned into gunstocks, wagon hubs,
oars, and shovel handles. By the late 1800s, billions of board feet of
timber were being converted each year into lumber for buildings,
bridges, ships, railroad ties, and the other gears and levers of this
new culture. The settlers were ruthless in their zeal to conquer the
landscape, and used their axes unceasingly to cut back the dark
wilderness that they feared harbored savages and wild beasts.

The juggernaut rolled westward over terrain that millennia ago
had been condor country. Pioneers plowed the prairies until today
only small islands of native grasses remain in what was once a lim-
itless sea. Along with changing the land, they decimated the seemingly endless herds of bison. By the 1880s, when most of the condor
study skins at the Berkeley museum were shot, a meager six hundred bison remained. Along with the devastation to plants and
wildlife came an enormous human cost. The Native American population collapsed under the onslaught of war and disease and habitat destruction. Despite the sudden and profound devastation,
some animals that arrived with the Europeans thrived: the Norway
rat, the house mouse, and birds such as the pigeon, house sparrow,
and starling. These species reproduced ferociously, spreading
across the land like the common cold.

Until the mid-nineteenth century, the distant and hard-to-reach
west coast escaped much of the onslaught. El Pueblo de Nuestra

Señora la Reina de Los Angeles was still a sleepy village, and much of the coast looked like it did when Friar Ascension explored it two hundred fifty years earlier. Steep cliffs washed by the sea sheltered primal forests and grasslands where condors foraged.

Then millwright James Marshall found a yellow mineral in a millrace near Sutter's Fort. Soon hordes of tool-carrying men, hungry for easy wealth, rushed to the Golden State. As mining techniques grew more sophisticated, the picks and pans of the first miners were replaced by hydraulic machines that ripped apart mountains and polluted rivers. Joining the miners were legions of builders, farmers, trappers, loggers, and railroad workers who dammed the rivers and fenced and paved the land. They clearcut the old-growth redwood forests and drained and diked most of the state's wetlands. In a few short years, the new arrivals upended the ecological balance of California. El Pueblo de Nuestra Señora la Reina de Los Angeles became Los Angeles, a metropolis growing like a fast-moving brush fire. Progress was on the march.

In studying old pictures of miners and loggers and railroad workers, I marvel at how tough these men were, performing hard physical labor in primitive conditions. Perhaps that's why there's rarely a smile to be seen. But there is also a stolid, steadfast look in these sepia images that testifies to their determination to subdue this new land. To many of them, a giant condor simply did not matter.

The Gold Rush and its aftermath cost the condor dearly. The burgeoning population of settlers brought a host of problems for the birds, not the least of which were their new repeating rifles. The newcomers shot the big bird out of fear or ignorance or just because they could. They also set out to rid the land of predators, such as wolves and grizzly bears. They shot these large mammals in great numbers while simultaneously pursuing an aggressive poisoning campaign. When the Gold Rush began, fifteen thousand grizzlies roamed California; the last one was shot in 1922. Condors, being carrion eaters, fed on the remains of these hunted and poisoned animals. Strychnine and other poisons took their toll on the birds. But another century would pass before the danger to condors from carcasses containing lead bullet fragments became clear.

When one considers that the passenger pigeon—a species numbering four billion birds, whose enormous flocks poured over the horizon like aerial rivers—went extinct in 1914, it's a minor miracle that a bird presenting as tempting a target as the condor endured into the twentieth century. How did this huge, slow-reproducing, never-numerous bird survive? Its proclivity for remote nesting sites may have kept it hanging by a thread. But for those who cared, it was clear that by the second half of the nineteenth century, things were not going well for the big bird. Illustrator and naturalist James Cooper said that in 1855, after his first observations of condors in California, he saw fewer every year in areas of suitable habitat. He thought there was little doubt that unless protected, our "great vulture" was doomed to rapid extinction. At the dawn of the twentieth century, another condor observer, C. W. Beebe, ventured a more ominous opinion, claiming that the bird's doom was near and that the last individual would perish within a few years.

Disgust, indifference, and misinformation about condors led many pioneers to see the bird as a giant, disease-carrying buzzard looking to carry off livestock and small children. What is so curious is that while decades—indeed centuries—passed, our knowledge of condors remained stagnant. Only a few early naturalists found the bird interesting enough to shoot it for museums or private collections. But before the twentieth century, *no one* seriously studied the bird.

○

The battle to save our largest bird means so much to so many people partly because the condor symbolizes the grief and longing for all that has been lost. The bird provokes strong emotions not because the troubles besetting the condor are so rare, but because they are so common.

In the early twentieth century the size and rarity of the condor finally began to attract attention. Not surprisingly, this came at the same time that prescient thinkers realized the continent's seemingly inexhaustible riches were quickly disappearing. A new conservation movement emerged: Theodore Roosevelt worked to preserve and improve Yellowstone as our first National Park; John Muir fought to save Yosemite. And a few naturalists began to seek out condors — not to shoot the bird or collect its eggs but to learn about it. These small early efforts initiated a twentieth-century metamorphosis, slowly changing the condor's reputation from a reviled creature to a chosen species. The bird attained such special status that decades later the government spent millions of dollars to save it.

One early naturalist who helped foster the condor's transformation was William Finley, a pioneering bird photographer who worked at a time when most wildlife documentation was done by artists. Born in 1876, Finley gained a reputation as an avid conservationist. He fought against the slaughter of egrets for the millinery trade and became president of the Audubon Society. His friendship with Theodore Roosevelt and his photographs of important bird habitats helped expand the National Wildlife Refuge System.

In 1906 Finley discovered a pair of nesting condors in the San Gabriel Mountains north of Los Angeles. Finley got lucky. He spotted the pair in March, just as their chick hatched. Along with his collaborator, Herman Bohlman, he took magnificent photographs of the birds as he observed the chick's development. Finley and Bohlman found the birds to be curious and very tolerant of humans. The two men repeatedly entered the nest and even snapped pictures of themselves with the birds. In the summer, Finley captured the chick and took it to his Oregon home to raise it. Later, he donated the bird to the New York Zoological Park, where it lived for eight years. It died after swallowing a large rubber band that had been accidentally left in its cage.

Two years after studying the condors, Finley published a review of the information then known about the species. He cited shooting and poisoning as reasons for the condor's decline, stating that under these conditions, it was not surprising that the bird's numbers were decreasing. Unless given protection, he predicted, the bird would undoubtedly go the way of the great auk, a species that had already become extinct.

The new conservation ethic prompted some modest first efforts to protect the condor. In 1905, the state of California made it illegal to kill condors, collect live condors, or take their eggs. In 1908, a hunter received a $50 fine for shooting a condor. But these laws were hard to enforce, and the shooting and egg collecting continued. Noel Snyder estimates that between 1881 and 1910, a total of 111 birds and forty-nine eggs were taken from the wild. No doubt there were more that never got recorded—perhaps many more.

After Finley's research, a handful of other naturalists made modest efforts to study the bird, but progress proceeded ever so slowly. By the 1930s, some experts estimated that only ten condors remained. One of the most important of the early researchers was Cyril Robinson, the deputy supervisor of the Los Padres National Forest, who conducted a condor survey in the mid-1930s. He estimated that there were at least fifty-five or sixty birds remaining. The true number was higher—probably closer to two hundred—but Robinson's estimate meant that the bird still had a fighting chance. Robinson, along with businessman Robert Easton, realized that the Sisquoc and Sespe regions of the Los Padres National Forest were critical condor habitat. The two men enlisted the support of the National Audubon Society and, in 1937, helped establish the twelve-hundred-acre Sisquoc Condor Sanctuary. For the first time, condors had a protected habitat, but it was almost too late. Soon after the establishment of the sanctuary, nearby road-building projects forced many of the birds to leave.

Despite the first halting efforts to learn more about California condors, much about the bird remained unknown and misinformation abounded. A popular 1926 movie, *The Night Cry*, starring Rin Tin Tin, featured a mean-spirited condor who killed a herd of sheep.

Rin Tin Tin is falsely accused of the crime, but when the dog implicates the condor, the evil bird steals a baby from its crib for the movie's final showdown. One wonders if any of the movie's viewers questioned how a twenty-pound bird could slay a full-grown sheep.

The July 6, 1934, edition of the *Los Angeles Times* carried an unintentionally hilarious article about a group that made a condor-viewing trip to the Cuyuma Valley in Central California. An artist's pen-and-ink drawing accompanying the article depicts a gigantic flying condor carrying away a fawn in its talons. No condor has accomplished this feat—ever. Condors have claws, not talons, which have evolved for walking on the ground, not carrying prey like an eagle. The article recounts how the group saw birds with fourteen-foot wingspans. They even reported one bird with a sixteen-foot wingspan. Granted, they didn't have a tape measure, but that calculation exaggerated a condor's ten-foot wingspan by *two yards*.

Even as late as 1969, the *Los Angeles Times* ran an article about a proposal by the town of Bardsdale—a hamlet near where I lived in Santa Paula—to attract tourists by becoming a condor refuge. A photograph shows the Bardsdale School building with an image of a condor superimposed above it, leaving the impression of a pterodactyl-like bird with a wingspan capable of darkening the entire school building.

By the late 1930s, a consensus emerged that the troubled condor needed help. The National Audubon Society decided to sponsor a three-year fellowship to study the bird. They contacted Joseph Grinnell, director of the California Museum of Vertebrate Zoology, to direct the project. Grinnell, a distinguished ornithologist in his early sixties, was a firm believer in field research and was eager to oversee the project. He awarded the fellowship to Carl Koford, a twenty-four-year-old Berkeley graduate student with a passion for zoology. Koford would use the fellowship to research his doctoral dissertation. The fellowship paid the grand sum of a $750 yearly salary plus an additional $750 each year for expenses. In exchange, Koford would spend hundreds of days trekking through some of California's roughest terrain to study the condor. To this eager young zoologist, it sounded like the perfect job.

So it came to pass that on a chilly evening in early March 1939, Carl Koford left Oakland aboard the *Owl* night train and headed for condor country. He was embarking on a project of considerable significance: the first scientific study of the California condor. This would prove to be influential, troublesome, and life-changing.

4

Carl Koford's Sensitive Bird

CARL KOFORD MADE his way to condor country via Los Angeles, where he spent a week laying in supplies and meeting with people who knew something about the birds. His most important contact was wildlife photographer J. R. Pemberton. Pemberton had taken pictures of condors and knew where to find them. He was also a partial patron of Koford's Audubon fellowship.

Pemberton took the young researcher under his wing and helped him get off to a good start. Before dawn on March 12, Pemberton drove Koford to Ventura County, hoping to show Koford his first condor. Koford arrived in a flannel shirt, work pants, and hobnailed logging boots. A shapeless hat covered his close-cropped hair, and his serious eyes held a perpetual squint. The two breakfasted in Fillmore, and then Pemberton headed his car up the dirt road that switchbacked through the area's rock-strewn mountains toward Hopper Basin. The sun rose on green mountain ridges, roiled like a frozen sea. Scattered stands of oak stood out like dark verdant islands. From many vistas, the steep canyons looked as they did ten thousand years ago, but beneath the striated rocks lay pools of oil. Petroleum companies had built roads and drilled dozens of oil wells in the area. Some sections of road looked out on pristine wild lands, but just around a corner would stand a half dozen oil pumps nodding up and down, a disconcerting contrast of isolation and industry.

At 8 A.M. they parked at the end of the road, and Koford began his observations. Within five minutes, he spotted a large bird roosting in a dead Douglas fir tree. The bird had tucked its head under its wing, and Koford wondered if it was an eagle. But when the bird stretched out its orange neck, there was no doubt of its identity. Koford's field notes are typically long on description and short on emotion. But at this moment, even Koford couldn't resist an exclamation point, jotting: *Saw my first condor! —at 8:10 A.M.* Soon the bird spread its wings in the sun to dry. A few minutes later, another condor cruised overhead. The two men continued to watch the original bird for nearly two hours, until it took to the air, flapped its wings twice, and sailed across the canyon.

Pemberton had brought Koford to the right place: condors were everywhere. Throughout the day, Koford never found himself out of sight of at least one bird. At one point, six condors flew overhead. The air carried the tang of chaparral, and Koford found deer and mountain lion tracks in the soft earth. In the late afternoon, he packed up some of his food, cached the rest, and bid Pemberton farewell. He followed a trail down to Hopper Creek, passing within fifty yards of two roosting condors. Alone by the stream, he set up a simple camp. It was a routine he would follow hundreds of times in the years to come. His first star-filled night was clear, calm, and cool.

○

I return to the Museum of Vertebrate Zoology at UC Berkeley to learn more about Carl Koford's story. Archivist Karen Klitz leads me to a long row of metal cabinets that house thousands of pages of university correspondence. Klitz has managed the museum's archives since 1987 and knows exactly where to look in this wondrous time machine built from letters and field notes. In a bottom drawer, we find a bulging folder holding Koford's letters from decades past.

Next Klitz takes me to the library—a large conference room lined with glass-fronted wooden bookcases—to look for Koford's field notes. The bookcases are filled with original documents. On top of them sit mounted animal specimens and skeletons: a weasel, a loon, a set of antlers. On one wall hangs a lifelike pencil portrait of Koford's mentor, Joseph Grinnell. As I work, I feel Grinnell's quizzical eyes watching me from behind his rimless glasses.

Koford was an old-fashioned biologist: he believed in *observation*. And he followed what became known as the Grinnell Method, which emphasized that scientists' field records are their most valuable results. Grinnell believed that everything even remotely relevant needed to be recorded because of the difficulty in knowing which observations might later prove useful. During his condor study, Koford filled thousands of 5- x 8½-inch notebook pages. At first, his lines of right-slanting cursive script are large and a bit gawky, but as time passes, the writing grows smaller, tighter, more controlled. From the first page on, however, the notes are decidedly thorough and detailed.

I take the first volume of Koford's field notes back to the gallery area and find a desk among the rows of metal cabinets. Next to me sits the giant shell of a Galapagos tortoise. I open the journal and begin reading the handwritten script. It is early March 1939, and Carl Koford is headed for condor country.

○

When Koford began his grand adventure, he carried with him a letter of introduction from Joseph Grinnell, Director of the California Museum of Vertebrate Zoology. The letter begins:

TO WHOM IT MAY CONCERN:

Let this certify that the bearer, Mr. Karl [sic] B. Koford, is a Graduate student in the University of California; moreover, that he holds an Audubon Fellowship in the University, under the sponsorship of the National Association of Audubon Societies, of New York City. Mr. Koford's subject of special research concerns the natural history of the California Condor.

The letter goes on to ask forest officers, landowners, stock raisers, and others to offer assistance.

Grinnell may have felt a touch of envy for Koford. On boyhood camping trips in Southern California, Grinnell had watched condors. As a young man, Grinnell rode a sailing sloop to Sitka, Alaska, where he spent a happy summer doing field research on birds such as the marbled murrelet. He went on to become one of California's most respected ornithologists, and he took a personal interest in young Koford's research. In selecting Koford for the Audubon fellowship, Grinnell made a somewhat unusual choice. Koford had trained as a mammologist, not an ornithologist: prior to his fellowship he had traveled through the deserts of Southern California studying rats and mice. But Grinnell liked Koford's tenacity and attention to detail and had been impressed with his capacity for work.

Every few days Koford mailed batches of his laboriously handwritten field notes back to Grinnell for review and safekeeping. Grinnell read the notes, and in avuncular and chatty letters—he addressed them "Dear Koford"—gave his protégé encouragement and advice. An early letter admonishes Koford, "Don't spend time writing letters to me—write *notes*!" And Koford obliged. In just over a month, he recorded more than four hundred pages of observations. The young researcher spent March and April in the field watching condors. And then in May, everything changed.

○

When I lived in Santa Paula during the 1970s, a friend and I naively planned a backpacking trip on an unmaintained trail from Fillmore to Santa Paula Peak. My friend's wife dropped us off at the trailhead, and we hiked into the mountains. In those days, I had no idea I was tramping along the same trails Carl Koford had hiked thirty-five years earlier. It was a bright spring day in a beautiful wild place, and we were in high spirits. What could possibly go wrong?

Before long, our easy-to-follow trail disappeared into ferocious stands of chaparral. We spent the day thrashing through tough, thorny thickets that tore at our arms and faces. At times, the going became so difficult we were forced to crawl, dragging our packs behind us. Just before nightfall we found a creekbed with a pool of water and enough room to stretch out our sleeping bags. I was too beat up to sleep, and spent the night worrying that we were lost. Much to my relief, the next morning we soon stumbled upon the established trail leading down from Santa Paula Peak.

It took three weeks for my chaparral-scratched arms to heal.

This is the trackless wilderness where Carl Koford came to learn about condors. Condor country possesses an untamed beauty, but it is also an unforgiving land. A mistake here can be fatal.

○

Koford spent his first two months of research in the Hopper Mountain area, scrambling down creekbeds and crashing through brush to observe condors and look for nest sites. His only breaks were trips to Fillmore for supplies and to mail notes to Grinnell. He also made brief visits to museums and forest service offices. It was rough, lonely work, but Koford only occasionally allowed himself the indulgence of noting in his journal that he felt tired or footsore. Some nights he slept in an oil-worker's shack that served as his base of operations. Other times he camped in caves or under the stars. In a rare moment of humor, he wrote to Grinnell that it would help if he had a pair of wings, a mosquito-proof hide, an invisible cloak, and X-ray eyes.

In May, Koford took a six-week break from his research for a family trip to New York, where he visited the American Museum of Natural History. He left condor country pleased with the rapid progress he had made in his first two months of research. Equally important, he had established a good rapport with Joseph Grinnell, and his mentor seemed happy with his work. But what Koford didn't know — what no one knew — was that a few months earlier, Grinnell had suffered a coronary occlusion. Grinnell had kept his heart condition a closely held secret. He had taken a sabbatical, but that did not seem unusual. Koford had no reason to suspect anything out of the ordinary, but after only a few days in New York, he received shocking news: Joseph Grinnell had suffered a fatal heart attack. Less than three months into Koford's research, his mentor and advisor was gone.

Koford returned from New York and resumed his research under the direction of Alden Miller. Miller, who had been Grinnell's assistant at UC Berkeley, was a physically powerful and formal man who liked to wear suits and ties. Like Grinnell, he had an impressive scientific resume. Over the next several years, Miller supervised Koford's research, and later, in the 1950s and 1960s, they would become allies in opposing hands-on condor conservation.

In the next two years, Koford spent close to four hundred days in the field battling demanding terrain, insects, blistering heat, and freezing rain. During his first year of research, Koford did not even own a car, forcing him to depend on buses, trains, and lots of shoe leather. To get supplies, he often hiked twelve miles of steep dirt road back and forth between Fillmore and Hopper Mountain. For one man surveying such a large wilderness area, Koford made remarkable progress. Within weeks of initiating his study, he found active condor nests that he visited regularly. He gave the condor chicks names—Greta, Oscar, Herkimer—and snapped close-up photographs. He even fitted Herkimer with an aluminum band, perhaps unwittingly dooming the bird to an early death. Because condors cool themselves by defecating on their legs, a buildup of fecal matter can collect around a metal band and "glue" it to the bird's leg, creating an area ripe for infection. It is now never done, but at the time, Koford had no way of knowing that banding a condor might cause it harm.

Koford's field notes tell the story of a researcher repeatedly entering nest sites, handling chicks, and observing adult birds at very close range. Nowhere in his notes does the careful young scientist mention that his presence had any long-lasting ill effects on the birds. The condor in his notes seems remarkably similar to the bird described by William Finley in 1906: curious and not easily disturbed by humans.

Yet in Koford's final monograph, published in 1953, we find that his condor undergoes an amazing transformation. Koford describes a profoundly sensitive creature that is easily disturbed by the slightest human presence. This strange disconnect between Koford's field notes and his monograph begins with the third sentence of the introduction: "Because condors are easily disturbed by men, observations were usually made from a considerable distance . . ." Even a casual reading of his field notes tells a different story: Koford spent many days in very close proximity to the birds.

This transformed condor—Koford's condor—emerges again in the monograph's section on nesting birds. Koford cautions that a person coming within five hundred yards of a nest site can keep a pair of condors from their egg all night or prevent the feeding of a chick. He states that condors react with alarm to loud noises from distances of more than one mile. He is especially adamant about photography, insisting that it is impossible to photograph nesting condors without causing serious deviations from their normal behavior.

All this leaves me scratching my head. *Where did these ideas come from?* Consider this May 4, 1941, entry from Koford's field journal, when he and another observer visited a nest, filmed the birds, and examined an egg by shining a bright light through it:

> *We left Parking Place at about 8 A.M. and hiked to Whiteacre Pk. and #8 nest (arrived about 11:15). We candled egg, took forty feet of movies of adult at close range, and retired to a distance. Both adults soared near and we visited nest a second time.*

This was a typical field note. Despite frequent close contact with the birds, Koford never documented that it caused them any problems.

If the condor's numbers had not continued to dwindle, all this might be simply a perplexing footnote to our story. Instead, Koford's "sensitive condor" became dogma, driving the conservation effort for the next several decades and fueling later battles over how to save the bird. History became a hindrance, with Koford's condor paralyzing research. An easily disturbed bird couldn't be approached for study. It certainly couldn't be fitted with radio transmitters or netted for a captive-breeding program. Ultimately, because of the perceived risks of approaching Koford's condor, his conclusions could not be disproved. The position became a closed, circular argument allowing no dissenting opinion. In later years, Koford grew more strident, maintaining that people didn't realize the damage that they caused to nesting condors by looking at them from a distance of a *half mile*.

So, what were the origins of Koford's condor, and what caused the great disparity between his field observations and his public conclusions about the bird? From the very beginning, Grinnell, Miller, and Koford himself thought that the birds needed protection from "John Q. Public." They adopted a strategy of concealing the condor and avoiding publicity about Koford's research. This penchant for secrecy shows up in Grinnell's letter of introduction for Koford: "He [Koford] desires no publicity whatsoever . . . which would in any degree increase the hazards of existence for the birds." Early in Koford's research, a newspaper report about his work drew Grinnell's ire. Koford's Berkeley mentors opposed a commemorative condor stamp, worrying it would bring unwanted attention. Ironically, by keeping the condor hidden, well-intentioned people who would have found the bird wondrous and worthy of protection were kept in the dark about its plight. And those desiring to collect condor eggs or otherwise harm the birds were going to do so anyway. So why take this tack?

Grinnell, Miller, and Koford, as well, wanted to establish condor sanctuaries: large tracts of protected habitat where the birds could roam free of human interference. A start had been made in 1939, with twelve hundred acres in Santa Barbara County designated as the Sisquoc Condor Sanctuary. But Grinnell and Miller had set their sights much higher. They wanted the Sespe—tens of thousands of acres of prime wilderness near the town of Fillmore. A sensitive, easily disturbed bird helped make their argument for protecting areas frequented by condors. Thus, Koford may have allowed his supervisors to exert a certain amount of influence over his conclusions on condor behavior. He was, after all, in a subservient position—Miller addresses his letters to "Dear Carl"; Koford addresses his letters to "Dr. Miller"—and it would have been natural to respect his advisors' ideas. That is not to say that Koford didn't come to believe in this version of the bird, a position he held for the rest of his life.

Although Miller, Koford, and their allies would later disagree bitterly with hands-on conservation measures, they certainly had worthy goals: to protect the bird from human intrusion and to navigate the politics of creating condor sanctuaries. They viewed their research through this lens. As we'll soon see, the scientists pushing for hands-on management also made grievous miscalculations. In the stormy battle to save the condor, no one was immune from errors of judgment.

○

By mid-1941, not even a young scientist researching a rare bird in an isolated wilderness could escape the conflagration of war engulfing the world. Koford, a member of the Naval ROTC program at Berkeley, received orders to report to active duty in June. He became a naval officer and shipped off to train in Texas. His journal notes are characteristically cryptic: on one line he records his orders to report for duty; the next line jumps ahead to his return from war in 1946, noting without comment that he has separated from active duty and is headed off to view some color films of condors.

Koford devoted the first half of 1946 to concluding his research fellowship. Although he finished his research that year, he still had the small matter of writing his monograph. Busy with other projects, it ended up taking him seven years. He worked on the final drafts in Peru, and in early 1951, Koford sewed his final manu-script—what he called "the thing"—into a sack and airmailed it back to Berkeley.

It never arrived.

As weeks and then months passed, Koford sent increasingly worried letters back to Berkeley. Where was the manuscript? After five months of fruitless searching, Koford turned to his brother, a lawyer, who filed suit for $50,000 against the airline that lost the package. The airline suddenly became very interested in finding the missing manuscript, and two weeks later they managed to track it down. Nevertheless, it still took two more years before Koford's monograph saw the light of day.

After finishing the monograph, Koford followed his interests in mammology, researching animals in remote parts of the globe: Africa, South America, Asia. Aside from a few brief trips back to condor country, for the rest of his life Koford never again studied birds. But since no one else carried on his studies, he remained the world authority on the California condor. Decades after he had hiked into Hopper Mountain with a pair of binoculars and a box of groceries, anyone who wanted to know about condors went to Carl Koford.

Meanwhile, in 1947, Alden Miller and his allies won the long-sought victory for the establishment of the Sespe Condor Sanctu-ary. Thirty-five-thousand acres were set aside, and, in 1951, the sanctuary was expanded to its present fifty-three-thousand-acre size. This prime condor habitat now had protection from develop-ment and human interference, and the new sanctuary allowed no human entry in areas most critical to the birds.

O

During the 1940s, the San Diego Zoo developed an impressive captive-breeding program for Andean condors. They employed a technique called "multiple-clutching" where the first-laid egg was removed from a nesting pair. This tricked the birds into laying

CARL KOFORD'S SENSITIVE BIRD

another egg. By doing this several times, it allowed the birds to lay eggs at as much as four times their normal rate. Applying what they had learned about Andean condors to its highly endangered California cousin seemed to zoo officials like a logical next step. The similarities between the two species made the California condor an excellent candidate for a program to breed birds in the zoo and then release them back into the wild. Thus, in 1949, the zoo asked the California Department of Fish and Game for permission to capture two California condors.

The proposal incensed Koford. He argued that the already precarious wild population could not afford to lose any members. In a letter to the commission, he railed against the proposed "kidnapping" of condors. He recited what became his standard refrain: A person coming within five hundred yards of nesting condors risked disturbing the birds. He also feared that captive-bred birds released into the wild might be carriers of zoo diseases. He concluded the letter with a sentiment that would become gospel among many who opposed later captive-breeding efforts: "If someday . . . there is only one condor left, would it not be vastly preferable to see it soaring over the Sierra Madre than imprisoned in a city park?" In other words, it was better to let the species go extinct than to hold some condors temporarily captive.

Opponents also feared that captive breeding might become a slippery slope, diverting attention and resources away from saving wild birds and perhaps opening the way for developers to seize the Sespe Condor Sanctuary. Opposition to the zoo's proposal brought together for the first time an alliance antagonistic to hands-on condor conservation that included, among others, Koford; his former Berkeley mentor, Alden Miller; David Brower, then with the Sierra Club; the Golden Gate Chapter of the Audubon Society; and the McMillan brothers—two rancher-naturalists whom Koford had befriended. The National Audubon Society also joined the opposition, although in later years they did not always align themselves with the hands-off position.

Despite the controversy, the commission approved the proposal, ruling that capturing two condors offered more benefits than harm to the bird's population. The commission didn't agree with Koford's allies that taking just two birds would tip the balance against the species. The zoo began their attempts to trap condors, but bad luck and inexperience hampered their efforts. Meanwhile, Koford's group fought on. They persuaded the California legislature to pass a law forbidding the capture of wild condors for *any* purpose. This new law went into effect before the zoo had captured any condors—a victory for Koford's side. For years, this decision quashed any efforts to research whether condors could be bred in captivity.

We can only speculate how different the condor's story might have been if a successful captive-breeding program had been started in the 1950s. It was an idea thirty years ahead of its time. Ironically, three decades later, the San Diego Zoo and the Los Angeles Zoo were back in the business of initiating a captive-breeding program, but by then—with only twenty-seven birds left—their backs were against the wall.

5

The Stormy Sixties and Seventies

AFTER CARL KOFORD succeeded in halting any condor captive-breeding efforts, he traveled the world studying mammals. Interest in condors waned. A loose network of untrained wardens—or condor "patrolmen"—provided sporadic reports and occasional protection for the bird. By the early 1960s, concerned that each year fewer birds were seen, the National Audubon Society and the National Geographic Society mounted another condor survey under the direction of Berkeley's Alden Miller. With Koford unavailable, Miller enlisted the help of Ian and Eben McMillan, the rancher-naturalist brothers with whom Koford had formed a fast friendship during his final months of research. Throughout his studies, Koford had made a point of meeting with people familiar with condors; the McMillans, in particular, had impressed him with their knowledge of the bird.

Ian and Eben McMillan lived in Central California's Carrizo Plain, a desert area that lies between San Luis Obispo and Bakersfield. As young boys, the brothers spent endless days roaming this undeveloped paradise. Nature was their teacher. But one tragedy marred this otherwise idyllic childhood. One day Eben was playing with his father's shotgun, unaware it was loaded. His right hand was draped over the end of the gun when it discharged, sending a full load of buckshot roaring up the barrel. Doctors managed to preserve only a clawlike appendage. In looking at pictures of Eben, his missing fingers are never revealed—he always kept the ruined hand hidden from view.

The brothers grew up to become excellent naturalists, and Koford felt a comfort and kinship with these two strong, independent-minded men. The McMillans became key allies of Koford's when he opposed hands-on condor management, and the trio remained friends until Koford's death, bound together by their interest in nature and their love of condors.

If the selection of Koford, a mammologist, was an unusual choice for the first condor study, placing the McMillan brothers in charge of the early 1960s condor survey was even more unconventional. The brothers had no formal training in zoology or science—Eben hadn't even graduated from high school. But Alden Miller liked that they were self-taught naturalists who knew condor country. And he must have known that they would espouse Koford's hands-off philosophy.

The McMillans conducted their field research in 1963 and 1964. Their published conclusions were alarming: they reported a thirty-percent decline in the condor population since Koford's 1940s research. If their numbers were right, only about forty birds remained. With hindsight, it is easy to point out the flaws in the Miller-McMillan survey. They based their population estimate on observations by different people at different times. Their final estimate of forty birds was almost certainly too low. But even if the McMillan numbers were inaccurate, they raised awareness of the bird's terminal trajectory—and that marked a critical milestone.

The Miller-McMillan study made another crucial contribution. Koford had concluded his research with a laundry list of issues affecting condors. But he provided no quantitative data as to which problems were most severe. Was the condor population dwindling primarily because of accidents, poisoning, shooting, drowning, wildfires, or collisions? Or did they suffer from a lack of food? Perhaps there were reproduction problems. Koford offered no guidance. The Miller-McMillan report provides *analysis*. Food shortages? Not a

problem—they documented the plentiful food sources. Low reproduction? Data showed the birds were reproducing at their naturally
slow but steady rate. Mortality? Now *here* was a problem. The
McMillans make a persuasive case that the birds were being harmed
by shooting and poisoning.

Like Koford's—and in fairness, those of all the other researchers
at the time—the report contains not a single word about lead poisoning, the major reason condors were in such trouble. But then,
this problem was not obvious or easy to deduce from the data they
collected. Although Ian and Eben McMillan may not have pin-
pointed the exact cause of the condor's problems, they deserve
credit for advancing Koford's work and setting the stage for later
efforts to save the bird.

○

Very early one morning I drive south from Santa Cruz to visit Greg
McMillan, Eben's son. I turn inland at Paso Robles toward the
Carrizo Plain, crossing barren hills on paved and dirt roads on the
way to Greg's home. Several mountain ranges create a rain shadow
that forms the Carrizo Plain. The McMillan clan has inhabited this
ancient land for more than a century. Greg and his wife, Linda, live
in a solar-powered straw-bale house surrounded by fruit trees.
Their living room windows look out over the rolling, summer-
browned hills.

When I arrive, Greg is transferring two barrels of wine into his
wine cellar. I give him a hand. Greg's in his late fifties and looks a
lot like his father, Eben: reddish-blond hair, blue eyes behind his
glasses, streaks of gray in his full beard. Linda brings us chicken
wraps for the road, and we all hop into Greg's four-wheel-drive
Toyota and head into condor country.

Both Eben and Ian lived into their nineties, and their ranch
houses are still in the family. We pass Eben's home, which Greg now
rents out. Down the road stands the house where Ian lived. Greg's
cousin lives over the next hill. It seems that nearly everyone in the

area has a connection to the McMillans. I feel like I've gone back in time and that Koford himself might come striding down the road.

"You saw Koford many times," I said. "What was he like?"

Greg strokes his beard. "A private man. Quiet, soft-spoken. I remember lots of biologists coming to visit my dad. After dinner, they'd gather around the big fireplace to talk, and Koford would sit off to the side, not saying much. But when he spoke, everyone listened."

"What would he do when he visited here?"

"He liked the solitude. He'd work on his writing, and he'd hike a lot."

Greg points out the car window to a small, now-deserted wooden house surrounded by olive trees. "There's the cabin where Koford stayed. He spent a lot of time there in his later years. It's where he came in 1979 when he had cancer and he knew he was dying."

An hour later we're bumping up a deeply rutted dirt road, climbing toward an outcropping of rock called Bear Trap where Greg's father once viewed condors. Greg talks about the present-day condor program, and I feel the keen tug of arguments from thirty years ago.

"The Miller-McMillan survey was the last real fieldwork done on condors," Greg says. "After that, the whole condor program got taken over by technocrats. The knowledge of what we have of condors since then is from birds that have been captured and manipulated."

I ask what he thought caused the condor's decline.

"I don't know. There was a lot of egg collecting. A lot of skins taken for museums. I find it extremely difficult to believe the problem was lead bullets ingested by condors that fed on deer carcasses shot by hunters."

Greg drops the Toyota into four-wheel drive to navigate the almost impassable road. As we buck and sway up the hill, I happen to mention that the recovery program is at a crossroads.

"What do you mean?" Greg asks.

"It's hard to see how the program can succeed unless they find a way to prevent poisoning of released condors from ingesting lead bullet fragments in hunter-shot game. They're going to have to pass laws requiring the use of alternative ammunition."

I can see Greg trying to reconcile the current lead problem with his belief that lead poisoning was not an issue for the last wild birds.

"What about birds released in the Grand Canyon?" Greg asks.

"Big lead problem."

"But they don't allow hunting there."

"The birds roam outside the park."

"How do they know the birds get the lead from bullets and not from some other source?"

"Distinct isotopes characterize lead from different sources, so it can be shown that condors are consuming bullets. Plus, biologists sometimes have to flush bullet fragments out of the birds' intestines. And most of the lead poisoning cases happen in November, which corresponds with deer-hunting season."

As the day progresses, Greg offers me bits and pieces from his father's life. I ask him how long Eben stayed active in condor affairs.

"Until the last of the birds was captured. After that, it was absolutely unnecessary. What was the point? It was done."

It dawns on me that for Greg and his father, the condor's story ended with AC9's capture.

"My dad and my Uncle Ian didn't have degrees, they weren't biologists. So they were moved to the sidelines." Greg shakes his head and asks rhetorically, "What could they possibly know about condors?"

We hike up toward Bear Trap, a rocky promontory with several caves that once held condor nest sites.

"Do you ever see condors up in this area nowadays?" I ask.

"I don't go looking for condors anymore. It pisses me off to see them wearing radio tags."

As we ride back down the mountain, I think about Greg's father and uncle. The McMillan brothers cared deeply about the bird and devoted uncounted hours to doing what they thought best to save it. Then the government got more involved, and the McMillans, once respected as condor experts, found themselves replaced. Eventually, the brothers even turned against one another over differing views about the bird.

"They started writing a condor book together," Greg says. "But they disagreed over some philosophical point—I don't even remember what. A schism developed that forever altered their relationship. For the rest of their lives, even at family gatherings, they barely spoke."

As I think about the McMillan brothers and their condor battles with "technocrats" and finally with each other, another big bird comes to mind: the albatross.

○

Nineteen sixty-five, the year the Miller-McMillan Survey was published, marked the beginning of another promising development in condor conservation. An annual condor count called the October Survey was initiated to track the bird's population. Many trained observers in multiple locations simultaneously counted birds. The results they produced were estimates, because it was not always possible to know if two observers had seen the same bird. In addition, weather and other variables also contributed to the count's uncertainty. Nevertheless, the effort provided useful data. Not only did it show the overall trend for numbers of birds and where they were distributed, but by looking at the proportion of young condors to mature birds, it gave an indication of reproductive success. Although the numbers varied, the first surveys usually accounted for fifty or more birds. When the last survey was held in 1981, fewer than twenty birds were seen.

The first Endangered Species Preservation Act, which was passed in 1966, also had a significant impact on the recovery effort.

Now the U.S. Fish & Wildlife Service was obligated to monitor and protect the condor. They hired a young field biologist, Fred Sibley, to assess the condor's status. Sibley's biology background, combined with his capacity to cover great distances in rough country and scale formidable cliffs, made him an ideal candidate. At the time, a proposed dam project on Sespe Creek threatened the Sespe Condor Sanctuary. Sibley's first job was to evaluate the effects that building the proposed dam might have, given the consequent influx of people and noise.

Sespe Creek crosses Highway 126 under a bridge near the town of Fillmore. In the summer, the creekbed holds mostly sand and boulders; the trickle of water justifies the word "creek." But after a hard winter storm, the Sespe—as locals call it—rages down from the mountains, muscular and muddy, a full-fledged river by any standard. The proposed dam planned to capture this winter runoff in a large reservoir. The massive $90-million construction project would bring hundreds of workers into prime condor habitat. Once built, the reservoir would attract thousands of yearly visitors. Proponents made a persuasive case: the dam would offer recreational opportunities, control flooding, and, of course, provide jobs.

Sibley began his study of the dam's impact by scouting out condor nest sites and monitoring the birds, something that hadn't been done on a regular basis since Koford's research. Within a few months of Sibley's arrival, however, local residents defeated a bond issue needed for the dam project to proceed. The election came down to the wire, with opponents defeating the bond proposal— and therefore stopping the dam—by only a few dozen votes. The dam project failed largely due to fears of increased taxes rather than concern over protecting condors. Tempers ran high, with some claiming that "forty dirty black condors" were holding up progress. One frustrated elected official mused that it was a terrible temptation to go out and simply shoot the birds. Despite the grousing, and a few half-hearted attempts to revive the project, the dam never got built. The Sespe still runs free and is now protected as part of the National Wild and Scenic Rivers System.

For the next four years, Sibley trekked through the same demanding backcountry that Koford had traveled. Ironically, Koford and his allies—having generated support for the bird—took umbrage at Sibley's field methods. Like Koford, Sibley regularly entered nest sites, but now this violated the "leave-the-birds-alone" dogma. Ian McMillan, in particular, was unhappy with the nest visitations. Sibley remembers an uncomfortable meal at McMillan's house:

"Ian launched into a direct frontal assault over nest site visits," Sibley said, "When Ian went into attack mode, a person had two choices: either listen or shout back. Discussion became impossible."

○

One day in 1967, Sibley got a report about a young condor in distress. The bird had not moved from its perch for several days, and no adult birds were feeding it. Rather than let it starve to death, Sibley and some helpers spent a frustrating day chasing the bird through thick chaparral. When they finally caught the starving juvenile, Sibley took it to his house, where it gulped down three pounds of hamburger.

After a recuperative stint at the Los Angeles Zoo, Sibley returned the bird to the area where it was found and tethered it near a deer carcass. The young bird still needed feeding and guidance, and Sibley was hoping its parents would return to care for it. Two adult condors showed up, but they weren't the young bird's parents, and one of the adults violently attacked the juvenile. During the dustup, the desperate youngster managed to pull out its stake and fly away, trailing its leash behind it.

For the next several days, Sibley searched in vain for the young bird. A last, a strong odor led him to the body, hanging from its leash upside down in a tree. When Sibley reached for the bird, it sprang to life, taking a vicious bite out of his arm. Despite his injury, Sibley was vastly relieved. He had found the juvenile just in time. He returned it to the Los Angeles Zoo, where zoo biologists decided to keep the bird in captivity. They named it Topa Topa after a mountain range in condor country. No one knew it then, but Topa Topa was the first condor in what would later become a captive-breeding program. A lonely fifteen years passed before any other condors were brought to the zoo. Eventually, Topa Topa did breed and produce young. He still lives at the zoo, a strong, proud bird ready to take a nip out of your arm.

○

During the 1970s, biologist Sandy Wilbur succeeded Fred Sibley as the U.S. Fish & Wildlife Service condor researcher. Operating on the theory that supplemental feeding would help the birds, Wilbur experimented with putting out carcasses of deer and goats for condors to scavenge. Although the birds sometimes ate the carcasses, the effort failed to halt the species' decline. Realizing that a more intensive conservation effort was needed, Wilbur pushed for the independent scientific panel whose recommendations eventually resulted in the 1980 recovery effort led by Noel Snyder.

Meanwhile, throughout the 1970s, Carl Koford continued to roam the world studying mammals. He remained a vocal critic of the hands-on condor conservation program, which had been gathering momentum. As time passed, however, Koford found himself on the sidelines. No one wanted to say it aloud, but he hadn't worked with condors in more than thirty years. New information, along with the bird's ever-decreasing numbers, demanded new solutions. It was far too late in the day to leave the birds alone to recover. That approach simply hadn't worked. Despite his estrangement from the recovery program's scientists, whose consensus was that a hands-on effort offered the species' only hope, Koford held fast to his position. No doubt he would have been a formidable force in the captive-breeding battles in the 1980s, but that was not to be. In 1979, Koford fell ill with cancer. In the final days of his life, he often retreated to the solitude of the Carrizo Plain and the comfort of his old friends, the McMillans.

○

It is the end of my day with Greg McMillan, and we're following the dirt road back to his home. "I'll show you where Koford is buried," he offers. We pass his father's old ranch house, he turns the Toyota off the road, and we bounce across dry weeds to the top of a low hill. We get out of the car, and he points into the distance. "My dad buried Koford's ashes at the spot where that telephone pole and that fence line up. There's no formal gravestone, but I think we can find the spot." After a brief search, we locate the burial site marked with a cairn of six stones the size of condor eggs. There are scattered clumps of wild oats and blue curl nearby. Here is where Greg's father dug Koford's grave, shoveling the arid earth with his one good hand.

Greg asks me to take a picture. He and his wife, Linda, stand in front of Koford's final resting place, their arms on each other's shoulders, and gaze at me with wistful expressions. Behind them, a melancholy milky haze hangs over the sandstone cliffs and parched hills that stretch to an enormous horizon. We stand wordless for a few moments. I am sure that Carl Koford would like this gravesite selected by his friend Eben McMillan. It's wild and austere—and it is in condor country. As we walk to the car, Greg says something to me over his shoulder, but the vastness of this land swallows his words.

6

Death of a Chick

I LEAVE TUCSON shortly after dawn and drive east across the Arizona desert on Interstate 10. I have arranged to meet Noel Snyder in his hometown of Portal, a hamlet three hours away in the southern part of the state. I love traveling through this expansive country of boundless horizons, where distance becomes a mirage. It is late summer—the end of monsoon season—and this morning I count more than thirty rain squalls circling the horizon. They create an aerial Stonehenge, with alternating columns of dark rain broken by luminous shafts of sunlight. Later, when I'm telling Snyder how beautiful it was, both of us struggle to remember the scientific name for rain that doesn't reach the ground. *Virga.*

Snyder meets me at the Portal Store & Cafe. The store is no bigger than a decent-sized living room, but it's the kind of place where you can buy oranges and tomatoes, a can of WD40, a book, a hat, a bag of flour, or a hummingbird feeder. There's a single fire truck parked across the road. Although I can see a handful of other buildings scattered among trees and desert scrub, the store appears to be the town's only commercial business. Up the road, the American Museum of Natural History's Southwestern Research Station lures scientists and scholars to this remote location.

It's a warm, cloudy day, and Snyder wears an open-neck shirt and still sports his trademark beard. We sit at one of the picnic benches outside the store and spend the next seven hours discussing condors. As the sun arcs across the sky, we shift locations to follow the shade. Snyder interrupts his soft-spoken sentences with frequent laughter. Since this is the heart of downtown Portal, a number of times people stop to say hello or to ask directions. Snyder seems to know everyone.

It isn't long before we're talking about Carl Koford.

"I respect people who put in the field time," Snyder says, "and Koford was a beaver. He worked very hard dealing with incredible obstacles. His field notes are so thorough, it's overwhelming how much information he recorded. And because so little was known about condors, he was inventing what he needed to do as he went along."

I decide to plunge right in with the big question.

"Why is there such a disconnect between Koford's field notes, where he routinely visits condor nests, and how he portrays the bird in his monograph, as well as in interviews and other writings later in his life?"

"Koford was in and out of nests like a yo-yo."

"Exactly. And with no ill effects. And yet he draws the conclusion that condors are easily disturbed. Why this disparity?"

"I wasn't there, so the best I can do is offer a hypothesis. Koford and his Berkeley advisor, Alden Miller, had an agenda. From the very beginning, they wanted to establish a condor sanctuary in the Sespe. And let's face it, they had a lot of opposition. You've got all those oil people who want to develop the Sespe. They faced an uphill battle."

Snyder chooses his words carefully. "When you have levels of uncertainty about information, you can sometimes select where on the spectrum you want to be. If you are going to estimate the number of condors left in the world . . ."

I smile. "If you choose high, it doesn't help your argument for a sanctuary."

"That's right. If you read Koford's original thesis, he says the number of condors left is sixty. He goes on to say, 'But if there are one hundred condors left, so much the better for the species.' Interestingly, that last sentence got left out of his published monograph."

"Miller's influence?"

"Miller may have been pushing him."

"Was it possible for Koford to get an accurate condor count?"

"He was one guy. A few times he had some help counting, but there was no way he could pick up all the condors. But he came out with the number sixty, and it became gospel."

"How many condors do you think were left when Koford made his estimate?"

"Once we had an exact count of the remaining birds in 1982, we looked at flock sizes in various areas, did an analysis, and compared the whole condor range back through time. We came up with a rough estimate of one hundred fifty birds during Koford's time. Maybe even two hundred. So it looks like Koford was way under the mark. Maybe he was doing it because of Miller. You can see how Miller might have been thinking, 'If we're going to get a sanctuary, we can't have too many condors out there.' Now that's speculation, but it's not unreasonable. And if you want a sanctuary, then other things also fall in place, such as portraying the condor as easily disturbed by human presence." He smiles. "But they did get the Sespe Condor Sanctuary."

"But as a result, the condor became an untouchable bird."

"Because the condor was so 'sensitive,' you couldn't study it. But if you wanted to understand the condor's problems, you needed to do some research. That's what we were attempting to do."

Talking about Carl Koford brings up the McMillan brothers, who opposed almost everything Snyder did during the 1980s. I ask Snyder for his thoughts on them.

Snyder smiles again. "Even though they were really on our case and could be rather angular at times, I have tremendous warm feelings for the McMillans. If you go back through all the people who theorized about the condor's decline, the McMillans came closest to the truth."

"You mean with the 1960s survey they did with Alden Miller?"

"Yes. They were right in concluding that excessive mortality was the condor's main problem. They just had the wrong mortality factor. But they didn't know anything about lead poisoning. And how would they? No one was testing carcasses for lead in those days. They got sidetracked thinking it was shooting or a poison used on ground squirrels."

"And they had no formal training."

"They were ranchers, not biologists, but they acted out of good common sense. Compared to everyone else, they were pretty close to the truth, so give them credit. They were doing their best to save the bird."

Snyder shakes his head. "As unpleasant as it is, programs benefit from controversy. And we sure had our share of it. Controversy forces issues to get looked at. If you create a closed system where everyone has the same point of view, it's a big mistake. You need opposition. You want to maximize different points of view. We all go into situations making assumptions. And no one has all the answers."

Later, the conversation turns to Snyder's arrival in California in 1980 and his first few months with the program. He tells me the story of examining AC9 at his nest site when the bird was two months old.

"AC9 was very docile. Handling him was deceptively easy and gave us no cause for concern."

"And then you visited the second nest site two days later."

"Yes. And it turned out to be a catastrophe."

○

Data is the lifeblood of science. If you're a scientist, no matter what you think of the results, you learn not to attach an adjective to the word. There are not "good" or "bad" data. Because science is rational and empirical, data are simply data.

In 1980, before the new recovery effort could begin, Snyder and his team had to know what was wrong and why the population was falling. And that meant collecting information. At the time, no solid data existed to explain conclusively the condor's dwindling numbers. Many people had strong opinions on what was wrong, but no one had proof. Noel Snyder's basic argument was that without hard evidence, any proposed solutions would be ineffectual.

An obvious first step in the hands-on approach was visiting nest sites to examine and measure chicks and to gather data on their development. These nest-site visits were only one part of a much larger data-gathering plan that included fitting some of the wild birds with tiny radiotelemetry devices. With radio tracking, biologists could at last see where the birds went. They could also retrieve dead birds to find out what was killing them. There were other plans as well, including the capture of a pair of wild condors to attempt the first breeding in captivity.

Snyder and his team had been successful in convincing the California Fish and Game Commission to grant permits, giving the program the final go-ahead for a more hands-on management strategy. Now the real work began. In the spring of 1980, there were only two active condor nest sites known to exist. Noel Snyder and John Ogden from the National Audubon Society planned to visit both of them.

○

When AC9 was still less than two months old, his world turned upside down. It happened late on a warm June morning in 1980. AC9 was dozing in the cave's coolness while overhead the sun bore down from an opaque sky. By now his downy feathers had grown longer and darkened, but the tips still remained white, creating a pale halo around his body. The first hint of trouble came with unfamiliar noises in the canyon below. The sounds grew nearer—large bodies picking their way up the steep embankment. And human voices. AC9 awakened and skittered into the dark recesses of the cave.

The sounds of the invaders drew very close. In the larger of the two cave entrances, a man with a beard and hat appeared.

Then another man. And a third. AC9 hunkered down. He waited and watched.

○

On the day AC9's world changed, Snyder, Ogden, and recovery team member Bill Lehman set out at midmorning from the observation post across the canyon and trekked cross-country toward AC9's nest cave. Veteran nature photographer Jeff Foott accompanied them to film the visit. Although it was a tough hike, at least the nest could be reached without rope work. They called it a "walk-in site," although "scramble" might be a better word.

As they approached the twin cave entrances, Snyder had a spectacular view down the canyon: dark-green oaks, gray-green chaparral, and buff-red sandstone. The spicy scent of sage mixed with the acrid odor of whitewash splashed on the rocks. A wrentit called from its hidden perch.

The biologists found AC9 crouching at the rear of the cave. Lehman caught the chick by the head and easily subdued him. AC9 resisted, but they handled him carefully, and he calmed down. Soon the bird was sitting quietly, docile and yawning, while the men took his measurements. With gloved hands, Lehman held the chick, while Ogden used calipers to measure his beak and head. They searched his feathers for parasites and measured his wings, feathers, legs, and feet. To weigh him, they inserted the young bird head-first into a feedbag and attached it to a hanging scale. The adult birds were nowhere to be seen.

Finally, Snyder took a trowel and methodically sifted the contents of the cave floor through a sieve box, looking for eggshells and other debris that might yield more data on nesting condors. A swirl of dust motes filled the air. Snyder's sifting produced several eggshell fragments. Later, these would be measured for thickness and tested to see if the birds had been exposed to toxins such as DDT. Snyder also collected several adult condor feathers that were scattered about the cave floor. These might also yield valuable clues about the birds' health.

Snyder's group stayed about an hour. The nest-site inspection had gone smoothly, and there was no reason to think anything different would happen when they visited the second nest site two days hence. No, there was no reason to worry at all.

○

Even today, Jan Hamber still recalls with sadness what happened on June 30, 1980, when the recovery team went to inspect the second young bird, a condor known as the Santa Barbara chick. This was Jan's nest site, and she knew the parent birds better than anyone. In telling the story, her voice grows soft and at one point she wipes her eyes.

"It was horrible. You talk about the highs and the lows, this was one of the terrible lows." She falls silent, and I find myself wondering about Jeff Foott, the nature photographer who filmed all that happened that day.

"What about the film?" I ask. "Is it still around?"

"We have a copy in the museum library."

Jan tracks down the film, but finding a working 16-mm projector proves more challenging. With the help of museum staff, we cobble together a projector: a lamp from one, a lens from another. But when we sit down in the museum's theater to view it, the projector's broken volume control only plays on "maximum." Because the movie has no soundtrack, the projector spits out a machine-gun-like roar. We plug our ears and travel back in time to late June 1980.

○

The first faded, jittery images show climber Bill Lehman descending the seventy-five-foot cliff to the nest site. It is immediately obvious why the less-experienced Lehman is making the inspection, and not Snyder or Ogden. He's the only one with the skill to rope down this brush-covered cliff in the San Rafael Wilderness. As Lehman carefully lowers himself, you can see his long sideburns jutting out from under a hardhat and sweat running down his face. He's wearing a plaid shirt, jeans, and heavy climbing boots. Strapped to his back hangs a bulging blue pack filled with equipment. A large sieve for sifting the cave's dirt floor dangles awkwardly from the pack.

It has taken Snyder's crew all morning to get prepared. Jan has been up since 4:45 A.M. in order to pick up other team members, drive to the remote area, and hike in to the nest site. By 11:30 A.M. she and three other observers are at an observation post across the canyon from the nest site. The setup is perfect. The parent condors are nesting in a large open cave that is about fifteen feet high. From the observation point, the crew can see every detail of the wide shelf in front of the cave.

By early afternoon, three men stand on top of the cliff above the nest site: Snyder, John Ogden, and rope tender Gary Falxa. Below them, Bill Lehman and photographer Jeff Foott are making the dizzying descent. Jan watches the two climbers through her spotting scope and tells herself there's nothing to worry about. Snyder and Ogden are very experienced biologists. Between the two of them, they have examined hundreds of chicks from different bird species. Carl Koford also repeatedly handled several condor chicks with no problem. And Lehman helped with the nest inspection of AC9 two days earlier and knows what to expect.

The chick sits alone in the cave. Her parents are gone, and she is unaware of what awaits her. As the climbers get close to the cave entrance, they toss a rope in front of the opening. The sudden movement startles the chick. She jumps back into a corner of the cave and lowers her head in a threat position. Lehman swings himself into the cave, standing upright in the wide opening. Heavy whitewash coats the inside of the chamber, and the hot stone reeks of ammonia. The only sound is the hypnotic drone of insects. Lehman calls up the cliff to Snyder, saying that the chick looks bigger than AC9 and has more feather development. He scrambles over to the bird, but the feisty chick spreads her wings, hisses, and strikes at him several times with her open bill. Lehman has no one to help him—the men with the most knowledge are standing on top of the cliff.

At last, Lehman manages to grab the chick's head and hold her down. His first task is to weigh her, and right away he has a problem. The gangly youngster is much too big to fit in the feedbag he used for AC9. After several minutes of struggling with the bird and the feedbag, Lehman crams her in his backpack and hangs the whole assembly from a hand scale. She weighs 6.4 kilograms: fourteen pounds of squirming, biting resistance.

When the chick slips out of the backpack, Lehman loses his grip. The bird retreats to the back of the cave. Now she grows even more hostile, and Lehman once again grabs her head to subdue her. He manages to measure her more than two-foot-long wings and notes the extensive feather development.

Across the canyon Jan watches Lehman's difficulties and thinks, *It's not going well.* She tries to reassure herself that she has never seen a bird this big examined, and that this is normal. But the struggle intensifies. To try to calm the bird, Lehman wraps a piece of cloth over the chick's head like a hood, but the chick shakes it off. Jan thinks, *I can't stand looking at this*, but her eye remains riveted to the spotting scope. The last measurement Lehman needs is the head. He succeeds in holding the bird between his legs and fits the calipers over the bill: 5.24 centimeters.

The camera zooms in close, and you can see the chick's head on the floor of the cave between Lehman's knees. The chick begins to pant. Its tongue lolls out, and its head wobbles. The bird goes limp.

Lehman calls out that something is wrong. On top of the cliff, Snyder rubs his hand through his beard and furrows his forehead. He doesn't like what he's hearing, but there's nothing he can do. Through her scope, Jan sees the chick on the cave floor, unmoving. She touches her Mickey Mouse hat, her talisman. She doesn't dare stop watching. Jeff Foott, who has been filming from a few yards away, drops his camera and runs to help. The film flickers to black.

Jan fills me in on the rest. In the cave, the bird isn't breathing. There's no pulse. Lehman bends over the chick and sprinkles some water on its head. He lifts up her limp neck, but the chick doesn't respond.

The frantic activity slows and freezes into a tableau: Lehman and Foott sit and stare at the chick's body. Jan puts her head in her hands. She can't bear to watch any more. After what seems an eternity, Lehman places the chick's body in the backpack, and Snyder hauls it up the cliff. Everything seems to move in slow motion. Lehman remains in the cave, dissolutely sifting the cave floor for eggshells for DDT analysis. On the way up the cliff, the backpack catches on some brush, but Snyder manages to untangle it. Once on top, Snyder removes the dead chick from the backpack and examines the body. No one says a word.

The crew carries the chick back to the observation point, and Snyder lays the body on a blue tarp. The entire team gathers around. They are looking at one of only two known California condor chicks in the world. And because of what they have done, this one is dead.

Jan begins writing in her field notes: "I had no idea it would be so soft. It's covered with incredibly long dark-gray down with whitish tips and has a round, roly-poly body with huge turkey-like feet. Noel is so depressed by the sudden turn of events. The political repercussions of this could be disastrous for the program. It's a terrible mess."

Everyone knows what this means for the recovery program: a firestorm awaits them. Finally, Snyder looks up and tells the group that the next step is to get the chick to the San Diego Zoo to do a necropsy. Bad as it is, they need to know exactly why the bird died. And they have to put out a press release and tell the world. Slowly the team gathers their gear for the hike out. For a long time Snyder remains sitting by the tarp, his chin resting in his hand, staring at the dead chick.

Jan stays behind at the observation post after Snyder and the team leave, watching to see what happens when the adult birds return. An hour later, one of the parent birds circles in from the east and hops into the empty cave, expecting to find its chick. It walks to the back of the cave where the chick often rested and peers around. It stands at the edge of the platform and cranes its neck, looking up and down the cliff, then off to the sides. It's as if Jan can see the wheels going around in the bird's head: *Where is my chick?* The scene breaks Jan's heart. The parent condor lingers at the nest site for more than an hour, and then flies away.

The next day Jan watches the nest site while the parent condors continue the futile search for their chick. She records their activities as she has done so many times in the past. She writes in her field notes: "It's depressing to see the cave so empty."

Jan stays one more night. The following morning, with rain clouds moving in from the west, she breaks camp. She stores her remaining food and zips up the sleeping bags and tent. She writes: "I don't know where the research will go from here, so am leaving most of camp until we find out."

She heads down the trail with a heavy heart. Her last entry in the field notes reads: "I wonder what will happen now?"

○

After she finishes the story, Jan says, "Would you like to see the chick?"

"It's here?" I am astonished.

"It was kept for a while in a freezer and eventually was mounted. We don't display it for the public, but you can see it back in the lab area."

We find the Santa Barbara chick stored on top of a seven-foot-high navy-gray cabinet. It is wedged between some cardboard boxes. I stand on a chair and come face to face with the bird that derailed the recovery program. It's entombed in a glass case roughly a yard square. Frozen in time, the chick spreads its wings defiantly. It is bigger than the large geese that frequent golf courses and urban lakes. Its body is solid and stocky, and its head is thrust forward aggressively. Long soft down frosted with white covers its body. The ragged and still-forming flight feathers look like a snaggle-toothed child's half-grown permanent teeth. Its feet are huge.

I reach up and touch a printed card on the glass that reads: CALIFORNIA CONDOR *GYMNOGYPS CALIFORNIANUS* SANTA BARBARA FEMALE. The small sign leaves so much unsaid. In all the years of the condor recovery effort, this was the only chick that ever died from being handled. It could not have come at a worse time.

○

Noel Snyder packed the dead chick in ice and the next day flew it to the San Diego Zoo to watch the necropsy. The examination found a healthy bird of normal weight and size, with no evidence of pesticide exposure, parasite infestation, or any other problem that might have led to its death. The zoo veterinarians laid the blame squarely on the recovery team: handling the chick caused it to die from shock and acute heart failure. The hands-off advocates' direst predictions had come true. The dead body furnished grim proof that the condor was a bird too sensitive for manipulation.

The chick's death made front-page news across the country. The *Los Angeles Times* headline read: "Death of Condor Chick Puts Program Into Turmoil." The *New York Times* headline was even more ominous: "Chick's Death Threatens Plan to Save Condor." The incident validated the arguments of those who opposed the hands-on management program, sparking a surge of opposition that turned the condor debate white-hot. The ghost of Carl Ko-ford—and the mystique of his highly sensitive condor that could not withstand human intervention—reared up in righteous indignation. The recovery team office in Ventura received dozens of angry phone calls. One person screamed into the phone line over and over, "Killers, killers, killers, killers."

Eben McMillan added to the brouhaha by wondering aloud if the recovery team had considered hiding the chick's death. He made an unsubstantiated claim that after the chick died, the crew discussed the possibility of a cover-up but dismissed the idea because too many people were involved. It's the kind of accusation that twenty-five years later still causes Jan to bristle. The chick's death was bad enough: the wrongful accusations only added salt to a very raw wound.

Eben McMillan also fired off a letter to California's Governor Edmund G. Brown, saying: "The recent fiasco, brought on when representatives of the National Audubon Society and the U.S. Fish & Wildlife Service invaded the nest of a California Condor and, through acts that could only be categorized as stupidity in the most basic of forms, brought about the death of one of the last remaining condors in our state."

Three days after the chick's death, Charles Fullerton, director of the California Department of Fish and Game, revoked all permits for the handling, capture, or captive breeding of condors. Never a supporter of the nest-site visits, Fullerton accused the recovery team of making serious mistakes in judgment and called for an investigation. Snyder's team was in full retreat and found it hard to justify to skeptics any further manipulations of the birds. The *Los Angeles Times* offered tepid encouragement in an editorial ominously titled: "The Day of the Condor: Is It Over?" The piece said that while they still favored human intervention to save the bird, the program must demonstrate that trapping the birds would not result in fatalities.

Snyder and others in the program remained convinced that despite the risks, collecting data offered the best hope for saving the bird. But there was no getting around the uncomfortable reality that just over a month after the final permits had been obtained, the death of the Santa Barbara chick had stopped the nascent recovery program dead in its tracks.

○

Snyder's official job description did not contain a section on worrying—but it should have. During almost seven years of running the program, worry became a constant companion, a weight he carried around with him each day. He worried about how to navigate the political minefields, and he worried about meeting the logistical challenges of the thinly stretched program. He worried about the race against time: the incessant ticking of the extinction clock running down to a final silence. Most of all, Snyder worried about his people. He knew that only good luck would keep him from losing someone. Someday a rope would snap or a team member would vanish on one of the "death march" journeys into areas so remote that the word lost its meaning. But a chick dying from stress at a nest-site visit had hardly even registered on his worry radar.

I asked Snyder about the difference between the two nest-site visitations. "Why did the examination of AC9 go so easily? What happened with the Santa Barbara chick that was so different?"

"What we didn't know at the time is that older chicks—like the Santa Barbara chick—are harder to handle. Much harder. They stress out a lot more than younger chicks or, for that matter, an adult bird. If you grip an adult, it goes into a passive state." He smiles and shows me a scar on his hand. "But you still have to pay attention."

"Losing the chick was a tremendous setback," he said softly. "A catastrophe. The miracle was that it didn't completely destroy the program."

○

As summer turned to fall, AC9 continued to grow and began to show signs of wanting to fly. The recovery team was no longer permitted to touch the birds, but they could still watch and take notes—and that they did with patience and persistence. AC9 was the only condor chick left; they couldn't afford *not* to follow him. By

October, observers were seeing the chick flapping its now-substantial wings for twenty or thirty seconds at a time, testing them against the wind. Typically a young condor will take its first flight, or "fledge," at five or six months of age. By early November, AC9 had gained enough strength and confidence that he was making flights covering several yards.

On the morning of November 7, the observer that day, Bruce Barbour, watched AC9 take several short flights. Barbour writes: "[AC9] looking down anxiously from his perch with wings partially open, obviously wants to fly down but can't decide where to fly to. He's inhibited." But by late afternoon, AC9 leapt off the ledge and floated out into the canyon. Barbour grabbed his binoculars. This was it—AC9's first real flight. Gathering speed, he sailed past the nest cave and headed up the canyon on wobbly wings. His feet dangled awkwardly. A young condor's first flights are not a thing of beauty. While juveniles may be nearly adult in size, they are gawky and clumsy and prone to crash landings. Sometimes they break bones or get stuck overnight within easy range of hungry predators. AC9 drifted higher, his unsteady flight carrying him toward the center of the canyon. Barbour watched the young bird cruise around a bend and disappear.

As the November night settled over the mountains, Barbour beat his way up the canyon after the bird. At last he spotted AC9 safely perched atop a large boulder. He watched until dark, and then spent a restless night at the observation post.

Bruce Barbour awoke to find a stiff wind blowing. AC9 hadn't moved. By mid-morning, Barbour estimated the wind speed at twenty-five miles per hour. As the wind increased, he watched AC9 repeatedly spread and test his wings. Then one of the gusts carried the bird into the air. He teetered his way back down the canyon, landing safely a couple of hundred yards south of the nest site. To Barbour's relief, the young condor did no more flying that day.

The next morning, a new observer, Gary Falxa, saw AC9's mother return. She had a full crop and proceeded to feed her chick.

The wind had died down, and the day turned unseasonably hot. In the morning, AC9 took a couple of short and successful flights. At noon, a deafening sonic boom rattled the canyon. AC9 crouched down, looking anxiously about. But as irritating as the sonic booms were—and they occurred with some frequency—they presented no danger. Falxa then noticed real trouble: a group of *fifteen* ravens had landed near the boulder where AC9 was perched.

Ravens are big, smart, aggressive birds with four-and-a-half-foot wingspans and heavy bills. One of them, bolder than the rest, landed within a couple of yards of AC9. AC9 went horizontal, lowering his head in a threat posture and turning to face the raven directly. Three more ravens joined the group on the rock. AC9 partially spread his wings, held them above his body, and charged at one of the other birds. He opened his mouth wide, showing his yellowish tongue, and hissed and thrust out his beak.

Falxa now counted seventeen ravens circling above AC9. The young condor hopped off the boulder to a rock shelf a few feet away. His parents were nowhere in sight. As eight of the ravens surrounded him, he hissed again and struck out at the nearest birds. His attackers answered with a chorus of raucous *kraaahs*. One raven approached within a couple of feet of him, striking with its bill. He parried back. Another raven landed behind him and nipped at his tail feathers.

Falxa watched the swirling onslaught with alarm. As AC9 battled back, he held the jet-black ruff at the base of his neck fully erect and lifted his tail feathers. The air sacs in his head and neck swelled, and he lunged at the nearest ravens with his deadly bill. The flock kept up their strident calls while they danced and dodged around him. Sorties of one or two ravens swooped in for the attack. One fearless raven came in from behind and again nipped his tail. He wheeled sharply on his attacker, ready to strike. The raven leapt into the air to escape the juvenile's sharp mandibles. More cautious now, the flock pulled back. Suddenly, none of them wanted to attack. And then, as if reacting to an unseen signal, they regrouped more than one hundred yards away, leaving AC9 alone on the rock shelf. Soon the ravens circled into the sky and disappeared.

AC9 remained frozen in position, still at full alert. It took him several minutes to relax back into his normal posture. Half an hour passed, and when the ravens did not return, AC9 launched himself into the air and flew unsteadily up the canyon.

7

Doin' the Double-Clutch Two-Step

AFTER THE DEATH of the Santa Barbara chick, even some supporters of hands-on management found their confidence in the recovery team's competence shaken. And, of course, the critics were howling. Noel Snyder took responsibility for the dead chick: he offered to resign. But the U.S. Fish & Wildlife Service remained satisfied with his leadership, and encouraged him to continue his work. A rough road lay ahead as Snyder and the recovery team tried to extract themselves from a political brier patch.

Snyder dug in and tried to regain some forward momentum with the token activities allowed by the California Fish and Game Commission. The recovery team continued to monitor the wild birds. They also tried to help nesting condors with a program to eradicate egg-eating ravens by shooting them. In addition, physical improvements were made in several nesting locations to increase the chances of breeding success. As ineffectual as these things were, it was all they had permission to do.

Even though the recovery team was now prohibited from capturing condors, the San Diego Zoo continued to build a captive-breeding facility. The Los Angeles Zoo, which already held the only captive condor, Topa Topa, also successfully lobbied for its own captive-breeding program. Preparing these facilities at a time when the recovery team was not allowed to touch condors proved prescient. Later, the two zoos were central to saving the species.

Snyder also tried to position the team so that it would be ready to act if the political climate changed. He traveled to Africa and Peru with Audubon's John Ogden to learn from other vulture experts. In Peru they met Mike Wallace, a smart young scientist researching Andean condors, who later became an important figure in the California condor reintroduction program. Snyder and Ogden were encouraged by Wallace's report that Andean condors—the California condor's closest relative—reacted well to radio-tracking, captive breeding, and reintroduction.

After his return, Snyder decided to try out some of the techniques he had seen in his travels. He took several recovery team members to a lake in Ventura County to test a cannon-net trapping device. Before trying it on condors, he first wanted to see how well it worked on common turkey vultures. They set up the trap, and several turkey vultures landed to feed on a bait carcass. But when the trapping team fired blasting caps to shoot the net over the birds, sparks ignited some nearby grass. The team tried to beat back the blaze, but the fire escaped them.

Snyder watched helplessly while a wall of flames roared up a hill toward an upscale housing development. It took 150 firefighters using tank trucks and aerial tankers to finally quench the blaze. In the end, one hundred acres burned, but to Snyder's great relief, no homes were lost and no one was hurt. He knew they were also lucky that no turkey vultures died. Had one of the birds been killed, the chances were good that cannon nets would have been prohibited, making it much more difficult to undertake radio-tagging and captive breeding.

Nevertheless, the fire reinforced the recovery team's Keystone Kops image as inept scientists flailing about making things worse for the condor. The episode provoked damaging media coverage and scathing derision from program critics. David Brower started calling them the "condor disposal program." Morale among recovery team members—already in the basement—sank toward subterranean.

○

In 1981, the environmental group Friends of the Earth added to the recovery team's woes by publishing *The Condor Question: Captive or Forever Free?* Written for the general public, the book presented thirteen articles and interviews assailing the recovery effort with a broadside attack on their methods and know-how. In the foreword, renowned Stanford biologist and *Population Bomb* author Paul Ehrlich wondered if the recovery team had not in fact come up with a model plan for *hastening* the extinction of the condor. I remember a friend showing me the book soon after its publication. Environmentalists whom I respected asserted with convincing authority that the recovery effort was the worst thing for condors.

Ken Brower wrote the lead article denouncing hands-on management. His father, David Brower, closed the book by recounting the hazards of disturbing condors and calling for habitat preservation. At the time, I didn't know some of the book's other writers — among them, the McMillan brothers and Berkeley's Alden Miller — but they, too, made the case that handling the birds was the problem, not the solution. The book included an interview with Carl Koford conducted shortly before his death. Sadly, it contradicted some of his own forty-year-old studies and perpetuated condor myths that were not based on research. Koford said:

> The [recovery program] recommendations emphasize trapping, marking, propagation, and release. But these dramatic artificial methods seem too expensive and controversial for efficient action. And their overall benefits are doubtful, whereas their esthetic and biological harm to the wild population seems certain.

Considering Koford's towering contribution to our understanding of condors and his own extensive handling of the birds, the interview did nothing to burnish his reputation as a careful scientist.

When I picked up the book again twenty-five years later, it was easy to see the lopsided arguments. None of the contributors had experience with radiotelemetry or captive breeding. Some had never worked with condors. And the book's subtitle missed the point: the choice was not between captive and forever free, but rather, temporarily captive or forever dead.

Ken Brower wrote to me recently that as time passed, he had entertained second thoughts about his earlier position. "We pretty much threw in with the Old Guard of condor people, led by Koford . . . old-style field naturalists against the radio-collar corps. We were suspicious that the L.A. Zoo and others would never release any of the birds in their clutches, and for a long time it seemed we were right. When they finally began to release birds, it was gratifying. (We had wanted to be wrong.) Not long before my father's death in 2000, I proposed to him, 'Maybe we were wrong.' He said, 'Wait until they breed in the wild.' And as I understand it, that has yet to happen in a substantial and reassuring way."

Brower is right: serious problems have plagued released birds trying to breed in the wild, and biologists are working to improve their reproductive rate. One thing is sure however; had the last birds not been captured, there would be no condors today—much less pairs in the wild attempting to breed. But back in the 1980s, the entreaties to leave the bird alone held considerable allure. For people like me, who at the time had only a passing knowledge of the recovery effort, the book's persuasive arguments were enough to give one pause. I am sure I was not the only one who felt dubious when I saw the recovery team's fumbles and their ineffectiveness in conveying their message. Many environmentalists—potentially their greatest allies—were filled with doubts.

During this frustrating, uncertain time when progress seemed illusory, recovery team members felt hamstrung to do something— *anything*—to help the birds. Even worse, everyone knew that another misstep could end the program altogether. The gloom only deepened when team members looked to the future and contemplated their impotence. If the species went under, it would be them, and not the California Fish and Game Commission, who would take the blame. The commission had given them just enough responsibility to be culprits, but not enough latitude to make a difference. The recovery team needed to show competence and regain their momentum. They needed a victory. But how?

○

AC9's parents—the CC pair—had started a new nest, but things were not going well. Condors usually change nest sites each year, and this time the pair had selected a location in the same cliff formation where AC9 was born. But the birds had made a woefully poor choice. Instead of a spacious, well-protected cave, they had chosen a cramped sandstone cavity, with a dirt floor that sloped steeply outward. At the slightest provocation, the pair's egg could roll out of the cave, cross a yard-wide ledge, and plunge to the olive-hued chaparral far below. At this nest, gravity was the enemy.

To make matters worse, the pair developed domestic problems. Normally, a condor pair shares incubation duties: when one bird rests or forages for food, the other sits on the egg. But the male, CCM, decided he wanted to be Mr. Mom. When his partner, CCF, tried to take her turn incubating, he chased her away. Only when his hunger pangs overcame him did he reluctantly give up the egg. Otherwise, CCM incubated for days at a time. CCF did not take kindly to this treatment. She asserted herself by jabbing at her mate's head and trying to push him aside to claim her rightful place on the egg.

One day, recovery team member Jack Ingram rose at dawn to monitor the CC pair. He set up his spotting scope from an observation post a third of a mile away. Ingram was a professional sound engineer who had adjusted his work schedule to join Snyder's coterie of around-the-clock observers. He worried that the poor nest site combined with the pair's bickering did not bode well for a successful hatching. Because of California Fish and Game Commission restrictions, however, the recovery team could not intervene, no matter how precarious the egg's future.

This morning, Ingram observed the birds begin another round of squabbling. CCM sat on the egg with stolid defiance while his partner eyed him with hostility, looking for an opening to take over incubation duties. CCF edged closer to him, then lunged forward and grabbed the egg with the hook of her bill. Ingram watched with horror as the egg began to roll, wobbling across the slanting floor and out of the cavity onto the narrow ledge. It came to rest just inches from the edge of the cliff. This time, CCM did not fight back. CCF strode to the egg and settled over it.

Soon, two ravens appeared, landing on a nearby rock and strutting right up to the ledge. One of them moved too close to CCF: she rose off the egg and thrust her open bill at the bird. CCM saw his chance—not to help his mate defend against the aggressors but to get the egg back. He sprang toward his mate. In the scuffle, the egg again began rolling. It teetered at the cliff edge for one uncertain moment, and then tumbled end over end down the sandstone until it shattered in a spray of yellow death. The ravens were there in a moment, gobbling up the spoils. Suddenly, one of the few chances the condors had that year of adding to their population was gone. A few minutes later, the condor pair joined the ravens in eating the remains of their progeny.

Would a condor pair that lost their egg wait until the following year to breed again? Carl Koford believed this to be true; here was a chance to find out if his theory was correct. Snyder, in contrast, was optimistic that this pair of condors would "double-clutch," or lay a replacement egg. Many other birds, including Andean condors, will lay a second egg, so why not CCF and CCM?

But CCM's aberrant behavior complicated things. What would he do now? Within twenty-four hours, he was spreading his wings and lowering his head in classic courtship displays. Attraction is a mysterious thing, and, amazingly, his mate seemed to forgive and forget their previous discord. Soon the pair was scouting out new nesting sites.

Forty days later CCF laid a second egg in the same cave where AC9 had been born. Unfortunately, CCM quickly reverted to his possessive ways. If anything, his aggression toward his mate intensified. Ingram and other recovery team observers watched with dismay as CCM repeatedly left the nest to chase CCF away from the new egg. The birds fought long-running battles, flailing at each other with wings and claws. The clever ravens noted the frequently unattended nest site. Three weeks later, as CCM chased his mate half a mile down the canyon, a lone raven landed at the nest, hopped into the cave, and plunged its heavy bill into the undefended egg.

At the time, the total condor population numbered fewer than two dozen birds, and the recovery team could ill afford to lose a single egg. In less than six weeks, two had been lost. The fights between the CC pair demonstrated that wild nesting attempts were not without hazards. Nonetheless, for the first time Snyder had proof that condors laid replacement eggs.

The discovery of "double-clutching" changed everything. A wild pair's first egg could be taken away and hatched in a zoo incubator, encouraging the parent birds to lay a second. Here was a workable method of building a captive-breeding program—with little or no impact on the wild birds.

Carl Koford once said, "The best thing that can happen to a condor's nest is that nobody finds it." This became a mantra for opponents of hands-on management. Noel Snyder and the recovery team proved them wrong. Thank goodness they had found this nest and discovered double-clutching.

○

Soon after Snyder arrived in California, an old acquaintance called to offer his help. Eric Johnson, whom Snyder knew from Cornell University, was now teaching at California Polytechnic State University in San Luis Obispo. Snyder enlisted his assistance in monitoring condors.

Johnson worked with some of his students to identify individual birds by their broken or missing feathers and organized a system for drawing wing diagrams of each bird's distinguishing features on three-by-five cards. He soon made an intriguing observation: like fingerprints, each condor displayed unique feather patterns. Since condors replace their feathers at different times and because their large feathers take four months to grow in, changes in appearance happen slowly. With fewer than thirty condors remaining, Johnson concluded it might be possible to identify every remaining bird.

One of Snyder's top priorities was an exact count of this very small population of condors. That was one reason why the recovery team wanted to equip the birds with tiny, lightweight solar- and battery-powered tracking radios. But with the permits for radiotelemetry rescinded, the team had no way to find out how many birds were left. The only other census method, the October Survey, had been disbanded because it was judged too inaccurate. Johnson's method provided a way to make the crucial condor count.

Snyder and Johnson spent months working out the nuances of feather identification. They soon abandoned drawings in favor of more reliable photographs. Observers using cameras equipped with telephoto lenses took hundreds of pictures, and Snyder and Johnson assembled an extensive condor photo file. It wasn't long before they had found all the known birds and assigned each of them a three-letter code.

Snyder and Johnson counted a meager twenty condors. One wild bird that escaped detection turned up the following year. Add in Topa Topa at the Los Angeles Zoo, and the condor's total population stood at a mere twenty-two birds. Although the low number boded poorly for the species, it eventually proved of immense value in convincing California's skeptical Fish and Game Commission to approve permits for more intensive management.

The Commission's ban on radiotelemetry, which provided the impetus for the photo census, proved to be an unexpected piece of good luck. Had only a few of the birds been outfitted with radio transmitters, it would likely have taken several years to acquire an accurate tally. The photo census accomplished that in just months. But the one thing the photos could not do was to track when birds had died. Later, when radiotelemetry was approved, the two techniques would complement one another.

The new photo census brought another discovery. In the 1970s, Jan Hamber had observed a condor pair that raised chicks in consecutive years. Carl Koford believed that condors produced a new bird only every other year. He wrote Jan a letter challenging her observations. At the time, because there was no identification method, Jan couldn't prove for certain it was the same pair. Later, with photos identifying all of the birds, her discovery was confirmed when a pair fledged chicks in successive years.

○

In 1981, one year after the Santa Barbara chick died, the U.S. Fish & Wildlife Service attempted to restart the stalled recovery effort. They filed an application to trap nine condors and to equip twelve more with radio transmitters. Once again, Charles Fullerton, director of California Fish and Game, opposed the request.

Fullerton was not a large man, but his silver hair and dapper wardrobe gave him an air of authority; he was a force to be reckoned with. In a windowless hearing room in downtown Los Angeles, the fate of the condor rested in the hands of Fullerton and five commissioners. Most of these decision makers had never seen the bird. The heated meeting ended with the U.S. Fish & Wildlife Service threatening to withdraw from the program if their request was not approved. The following month feuding state and federal officials finally reached a compromise agreement to capture three condors and radio-tag six more. But bureaucrats continued to argue over whether to attach the radio tags to the birds' wings or tail. Six months after the meeting, the recovery team finally received permission to capture birds. But it is not easy to trap condors. Despite their best efforts, bad luck and poor weather conspired against the recovery team. When the permits lapsed in May (the commission thought it inadvisable to disturb the birds during the summer heat), not a single bird had been caught.

To make matters worse, the commission subsequently tightened their already restrictive regulations, limiting captures to just one bird: a mate for Topa Topa. Unfortunately, Topa Topa had been raised around humans, and many questioned if he would display normal wild behavior. He didn't seem like a good candidate for captive breeding.

Time was passing. Birds were dying. And the commission would still not allow a hands-on program.

○

In the summer, the father of one of the year's few condor nestlings disappeared. Recovery team observers watched with concern as the lone parent bird struggled to provide enough food for her youngster. With the chick's future in jeopardy, Snyder's team gained emergency permission to capture it. They understandably had the jitters over the capture attempt. This would be the first time they had handled a bird since the Santa Barbara chick's death; losing another bird could spell the end of the recovery effort. Ominously, the operation was scheduled for Friday the thirteenth.

At midday, the team climbed to the nest site. This time, Snyder brought with him veterinarian Phil Ensley from the San Diego Zoo. Snyder had come to know and trust Ensley while the two of them were observing Andean condors in Peru. Ensley quickly corralled the bird and placed him in a portable sky kennel. It couldn't have gone more smoothly. No sooner had the young bird arrived safely at the San Diego Zoo than he downed eighteen mice. Here was proof that handling the birds caused no ill effects. Snyder could breathe again.

○

In the following months, the recovery team continued their attempts to capture their first wild condor with a cannon net. This was another new and potentially high-risk procedure where a mistake could be lethal to the still-tenuous program. Snyder again tapped Ensley to come along as the team's veterinarian. He also brought Pete Bloom, who served as their condor trapper.

At a site on Tejon Ranch, they built a crude four-by-eight plywood blind and camouflaged it with manzanita branches and limbs cut from valley oaks. More than one hundred feet away, they cleared an area for the bait carcass, and dug a shallow trench to hold the accordion-folded sixty-square-foot net. They staked down one end of the net like a tent and attached the leading edge to lines that went to four pipes loaded with blasting caps and metal weights. A detonator in the blind would electronically fire the blasting caps, shooting the weights and the net over the bait carcass. In order to avoid hitting a condor with one of the flying metal weights, they ran test firings to aim the blast tubes accurately. To be extra safe, they decided to fire the net only when a bird had its head lowered to feed. Snyder also made sure that they had canvas bags of water to douse any stray sparks.

Before dawn on October 12, Snyder, Ensley, and Bloom staked down a calf carcass and hid themselves in the blind. Three viewing portholes cut in the wall provided the only light, and the air smelled of earth and plywood. Once settled in the cramped blind, they dared not leave because they feared revealing their position. They munched on crackers and peanut butter, read, and dozed.

"We had only one rule," Ensley said. "No farts."

It was very cold, and Snyder drank tea to stay warm. They sat on uncomfortable folding chairs while the hours passed and no condors appeared. Snyder began to regret drinking so much tea.

Late in the morning, a spotter called on their two-way radio. "Condor overhead!" The bird circled the bait carcass for a few minutes before dropping out of the sky, and then cautiously approached the dead calf. Snyder flicked a switch on the detonator box, and in the blind's dim interior, the "ready light" glowed red. The bird lowered its head, and Snyder counted softly: "One, two, three . . . *now*." The blasting caps roared, and the net shot over it.

Now they needed to run the one hundred feet from the blind to the calf carcass before the bird freed itself. Bloom shoved the blind's door open, but the three men could scarcely move: they were stiff and numb from hours of sitting in the cold. The condor thrashed about under the net, working its way toward the edge — and freedom. The trio staggered toward the net. Bloom arrived first, but tripped on the rough ground and went down. Then Ensley took a spill. The bird heard their footfalls and struggled harder. Ensley dove the last few feet and pressed the net tightly over the bird. Bloom wrapped his arms around its wings. Soon, the bird calmed down. They had done it.

But where was Snyder?

"I looked around," Ensley said, "and Noel had his back to us. He had seen we had safely subdued the bird and was relieving himself of all that tea."

Ensley examined the bird, drew a vial of blood, and put it in a sky kennel. The trapping team was exultant at the successful capture.

"We felt immense pressure to do it right," Bloom said. "We all knew if anything went wrong . . . well, there was simply no room for error."

I asked Bloom what it was like waiting for long hours in a dark blind. "It isn't too difficult to wait for a bird as special as a condor," he said. "We were three of the luckiest biologists in the world. I remember right before we fired the cannon net, Noel turned to Ensley and me and said, 'It's a privilege and an honor to be here with you guys.'"

They drove the bird to a nearby weather station to wait for the results of the blood test that would determine the bird's sex. A female would be transferred to the Los Angeles Zoo as a mate for Topa Topa; a male would be radio-tagged and released. Two days later, they learned it was a male.

"At that point there was some politicking going on," Ensley told me. "Should the bird be taken in, even though it was a male? I think Noel was wondering why we would want to release a young bird that's four years or more away from breeding. Anything can go wrong in the wild. The bird would be safe in captivity. Noel was thinking: 'Bring him in to help start a captive-breeding flock—it's money in the bank.'"

But Snyder didn't win this one, and they were ordered to release the bird. On the front of his wings Snyder attached radio transmitters and white number tags. They called the bird IC1, Immature Condor 1. Then IC1 flew away, ignoring its new wing gear. A year and a half passed before Snyder would again handle IC1—under circumstances that were both tragic and transforming for the recovery effort.

○

By the autumn of 1982, several events coalesced that finally enabled the recovery team to achieve critical mass for restarting hands-on management. A crucial part of this turnaround was the double-clutch discovery, which made possible a captive-breeding program. Privately, Snyder was not 100-percent sure that double-clutching would work. "We had, after all, a sample of only one," he said. "But it seemed logical, and by the next breeding season, we learned that condors almost always double-clutch."

Other events also helped make a compelling case for the urgency of restarting the program. The dire numbers—a paltry twenty-two birds—revealed by the photo census, the neglected chick's trouble-free capture, and success with radio-tagging all added weight to the call to begin hands-on management. The National Audubon Society increased the pressure, announcing that it planned to withdraw funding from the recovery effort unless the California Fish and Game Commission issued the needed permits.

Finally, as if to compensate for all the bad luck and mistakes of the past two years, a piece of political good fortune fell into Snyder's lap. In a logistical meeting Snyder held with officials at the Los Angeles Zoo, the discussion turned to the larger issues facing the recovery program. The officials listened as Snyder described how the recovery effort's plans were thwarted by the commission's onerous restrictions. Marcia Hobbs, the zoo's fund-raiser, was politically well connected and eager to help. A goddaughter of President Ronald Reagan, she knew some of the California Fish and Game commissioners and decided to do some lobbying of her own. Snyder had been given erroneous instructions not to speak with the commissioners privately, so up until now they had only heard from him in contentious public meetings. But after Hobbs made some calls, Snyder suddenly found himself invited for one-on-one conversations. In these informal talks, the commissioners found Snyder's cogent arguments and obvious intelligence persuasive. Just a few days later, the director of California Fish and Game, the previously reluctant Charles Fullerton, came out in support of a new program approving the removal of all the first-laid eggs in 1983, along with allowing radiotelemetry on most of the remaining birds.

Snyder and the recovery team were back in business.

○

With permission to start captive breeding, Snyder now worried about retrieving the first egg. The recovery team had no experience performing this tricky operation, and there was not much information to guide them. In the past, scores of collectors had taken condor eggs from nests, but never with the intention of keeping them alive. Somehow Snyder had to slip past the parent condors, snatch the egg, and maintain its warmth and safety while transporting it by helicopter to a zoo incubator. Snyder had no doubt that if anything went awry, the whole recovery program could be again shut down.

Snyder chose Bill Toone from the San Diego Zoo to accompany him on the first egg retrieval. If the chick hatched, it would be Toone who would supervise its upbringing at the zoo. Toone, an experienced and articulate biologist, knew that success would give the recovery program a huge boost. He did not want to contemplate failure.

The nest cave lay in a narrow gorge of mottled sandstone cliffs. "We hiked in under the cover of darkness," Toone recalled. "Neither Noel nor I thought it necessary, but we did it to mollify critics who believed condors were easily disturbed. We climbed up this crumbling escarpment, where one misstep could have sent us tumbling into the gorge below. The next morning, when I looked down from our camp, I wondered if I would have had the nerve to make the climb in daylight."

Snyder and Toone set up their tent just out of sight of the cave and settled in to wait for the right moment to grab the egg. Nearly a mile away, observers with a spotting scope and two-way radios kept them apprised of the birds' movements.

A few days earlier, a recovery team crew cut a crude helicopter landing pad farther up the mountain. Snyder planned to carry the precious egg in a rudimentary carrier made from a foam-filled suitcase. Hot water bottles kept the interior warm, and two thermometers to monitor the internal temperature protruded from holes cut in the side. Once Snyder and Toone snatched the egg, they would climb to a waiting helicopter and fly to the San Diego Zoo. But the weather gods would have to be with them; 1983 was an El Niño year with frequent storms that made flying impossible. Timing the helicopter pickup was critical; if they didn't move quickly enough, the egg would cool and die.

But retrieving the egg presented the trickiest challenge. Incubating condors usually place their egg on top of their feet. If startled, they can stand up quickly, causing the egg to roll away and break. Records of an early condor observer described how he came upon a nest too abruptly and watched the egg careen out of the cave. Snyder figured that their best chance to grab the egg would be when the parent birds handed off incubating duties, leaving the egg unattended while they spent a few minutes flying together. Unfortunately, these exchanges occurred only once every few days.

While Snyder and Toone waited in their tent, the suitcase needed constant attention. "We didn't know when the birds might make an exchange," Toone said. "So the water bottles always needed to be at the proper temperature. We spent the day heating water and refilling bottles."

Night fell with no incubating exchange. Another day passed, and Snyder grew impatient. If the incubation exchange occurred in bad weather, they might end up waiting several more days. Perhaps they were being too cautious.

He decided to take a chance and try a bolder strategy. At mid-morning, he and Toone began walking slowly toward the cave. They talked in tones that would gently alert the bird of their approach, but would not alarm it. Upon hearing their voices, the incubating bird cocked his head and looked their way. As the men continued talking and moving closer, the bird rose—slowly—to its feet. Curious, it came out to look.

Snyder and Toone drew near to the cave, but the bird did not give ground. Would it stand and fight to defend the nest? The pair kept talking and edged closer. They were just three yards away when the bird finally took wing.

Snyder and Toone pulled on surgical gloves and clambered into the cave. Snyder's flashlight illuminated the bluish green egg resting on the dirt floor. It was two-and-a-half inches wide and nearly four-and-a-half inches long. They had practiced their procedure many times. First, they evaluated the egg, checking for cracks or damage. It looked healthy. Snyder breathed a small sigh of relief. If the egg was not intact, some recovery program opponents would blame it on their visit.

As they worked, the adult bird flew past the cave, darkening the entrance with each pass. It flew so close that they could look into the bird's eyes. The consequences of what they were about to do was not lost on the two biologists. Assuming that this was a healthy egg and the bird survived, it might spend decades riding the Southern California thermals. But if they took the egg to the San

Diego Zoo, it would live its life in an enclosure eighty feet long, forty feet wide, and twenty-four feet tall. Toone and Snyder exchanged a glance. Captive breeding was the only hope.

Snyder nodded. Toone picked up the egg and gently placed it in the incubating suitcase. It fit perfectly, and the thermometer showed 95°F: exactly right. Now the clock started ticking. Several miles away a helicopter was weaving its way through a maze of canyons toward the mountaintop landing pad. Snyder and Toone began their ascent up the dizzyingly steep hillside. Neither man was a skilled mountain climber, and both of them were terrified that one slip could send them and their suitcase cartwheeling to destruction. Even the jostling from a minor fall could kill the developing embryo. Snyder took several steps forward and found a secure footing. Toone handed him the suitcase, and then moved ahead a few more steps to another foothold. Snyder passed the suitcase to Toone. Slowly they worked their way upward until at last the helipad and the waiting red-and-white helicopter came into view.

Snyder and Toone roared skyward along with their precious cargo. They flew below five thousand feet so that air pressure changes would not harm the egg. On the way to San Diego, Toone thought again about how they were dooming this still-developing chick to a caged life in order to save the species. He made a silent vow to stay with the condor program until the first birds were released.

An hour later, the helicopter descended toward a makeshift landing site in the zoo's parking lot. Thus far the egg retrieval had gone well, but ahead lay several weeks of incubation and then the most dangerous time of all: hatching.

○

An egg, with its slumbering possibilities, is a marvel of design. The strong yet porous shell protects the embryo while allowing the exchange of oxygen and carbon dioxide. Snyder and Toone's prize now resided in a commercial egg incubator. This rarest of eggs received round-the-clock care. Zoo biologists monitored the air circulation and temperature and adjusted the humidity so that the egg did not dehydrate. The weeks passed, and toward the end of March, a tiny pip hole appeared. The chick's most vulnerable time had arrived.

But Toone and his zoo colleagues knew precious little about hatching a condor egg. They were not even sure how long it should take. A day went by and progress seemed agonizingly slow. Two days passed. Chicks can die from exhaustion trying to free themselves from an egg. On day three, they decided to step in. Based on what they knew from hatching Andean condor eggs, they did not want to let the chick fight on into a fourth day. They donned surgical masks and gloves and placed the egg on an operating table. With utmost care, they used forceps to break off a tiny piece of shell and then took a sterile spray bottle and misted the exposed membranes with water. After they broke off each piece, they "candled" the egg, shining a bright light on the area to consider their next move. While in its egg, a chick will breathe through an extensive blood vessel system attached to the shell. Break off part of the egg too soon and an artery can be severed, causing the chick to bleed to death.

It took hours of this painstaking work before the chick finally broke free. On the operating table lay an extraordinary sight: a baby condor, still too weak to stand. No humans had ever before witnessed the birthing of a newborn California condor, and Toone felt giddy with exhaustion and exaltation. This momentous event filled him with hope. The next morning, they fed the chick a purée of warm water and finely chopped day-old mice. Afterward, with the chick safely asleep in a terry-cloth-lined incubator, Toone and other zoo officials met with the media to announce the news.

"It was a shock to go from the sleepless intensity of the incubating area to a room filled with reporters and TV cameras," Toone said. "It was also a bit astonishing. The world was clamoring to know all about our baby condor. But one question gave us pause. The reporters wanted to know the chick's name. Incredible as it may seem, we hadn't thought to name it. We had assigned a letter and number designation telling the area of its birth, but with all the publicity, we didn't want to release that information. The last thing we needed was curiosity seekers searching for the chick's birth site. On the spur of the moment, we decided to call it Sisquoc, an Indian name for an area near where the egg was laid."

Within hours, baby Sisquoc made front-page news around the world. The seven-ounce chick gave the recovery effort a huge public relations victory. Suddenly members of the recovery team were the good guys. Congratulations rolled in. Even the Prince of Wales sent his best wishes. At last they had a victory.

That spring, the recovery team successfully retrieved and hatched three more condor eggs; all of the chicks survived. In addition, another wild chick was captured without incident. Things were going equally well with the wild condor population. Months passed and not a single bird died or was injured. For the first time the recovery team had momentum. In light of the program's successes, opposition to captive breeding faded.

Nineteen eighty-three was the best of times. With captive breeding supplementing the wild condor population, John Ogden from the National Audubon Society predicted that the condor would survive: "I think you can now say that we will never lose the condor. I believe we can artificially maintain the population in the wilderness with no problem. We could keep it at, say, twenty or thirty birds forever by resupplying the wild population from the zoos."

The rest of the recovery team shared his optimism. Only a year earlier, they had hit bottom, with only twenty-two birds left and no captive-breeding program. Now it looked as if the recovery team had pulled off the impossible. But with the condor, nothing is ever easy. Ahead lay what Noel Snyder remembers as the worst year of his life.

8

Point of No Return

NOEL SNYDER PEERED through his spotting scope and smiled in delight. A pair of nesting condors was inhabiting a most unusual location: a burned-out cavity high in a giant sequoia tree. Snyder had spent much of the day at this newly discovered site, far from the usual condor nesting grounds. It was early 1984, and recovery team members had recently tracked radio-tagged condors to Kern County here in this part of the Sierra Nevada foothills. The nest had been discovered just this morning, giving Snyder yet another piece of good news for the recovery program which was still riding a high following Sisquoc's birth.

Snyder was about to call it a day when an urgent message came over his two-way radio. The tracking signal from another radio-tagged condor a few miles away had stopped moving—and that meant trouble. Snyder made some calls and headed for the site of the stationary signal, a place called Blue Ridge at the edge of the Sequoia National Forest. With darkness closing in, it was critical to get to the bird before nighttime predators began to prowl.

The downed condor was IC1, the first bird Snyder had radio-tagged. That afternoon, a National Audubon Society pilot who was tracking condors noticed IC1's unmoving signal. When the pilot flew low over Blue Ridge, he could not see the bird—an ominous sign, since perching condors usually can be seen from the air.

Jesse Grantham, a recovery team stalwart, also got the call about IC1. He arrived at Blue Ridge before Snyder. As the light faded, Grantham used his tracking receiver to follow the radio signal down a hillside covered with oaks and pines. The smell of grass filled the early evening air, and Grantham's receiver clicked incessantly. Up ahead, he spied a dark shape sprawled on the ground. Although the bird appeared dead, Grantham approached carefully: he had learned to respect the condor's sharp bill. Cautiously, he lifted one of the bird's wings away from the body. *Definitely dead.* Grantham noted the mature white wing patches that had developed since he had helped Snyder tag the bird eighteen months earlier. In the dim light, Grantham saw no apparent reason for IC1's death.

Soon Snyder and other recovery team members arrived. Before moving the bird, Snyder wanted to look over the scene in daylight to hunt for clues. He had a recovery team member stay overnight with IC1 to protect it from predators. When he returned at dawn, the body was covered with frost. He saw immediately that they had a stroke of good luck: the bird's battery-operated radio was missing, but the solar-powered transmitter landed face up and was still operating, allowing them to find the body. A meticulous search of the area turned up no obvious cause of death. That intrigued Snyder. Towering over IC1's body was a dead pine tree covered with whitewash. It looked as if the bird had been sitting in the roosting snag and had suddenly dropped dead.

Snyder packed IC1's body in ice and flew it to the San Diego Zoo to perform a necropsy. The examination showed no bullet wounds and no predator teeth marks. There were, however, several broken ribs, but they were almost certainly a result of the bird's fall. In any case, these were not fatal. Something else had killed IC1.

A full-body radiograph produced a most interesting piece of evidence: a quarter-inch-long sliver from a lead bullet rested deep in IC1's digestive tract. Snyder's pulse quickened. He had long suspected condors might be dying from consuming bullet fragments in hunter-shot game. This appeared to be the first proof that condors were indeed dying from lead. Confirming this evidence was critical. He immediately called the U.S. Fish & Wildlife Service pathologist in Wisconsin, the expert in such matters. The pathologist boarded the next plane to California.

One look at the radiograph and the pathologist confirmed their suspicions: lead was almost certainly the cause of death. Sure enough, later lab results from tissue and blood samples showed toxic lead levels. Lead poisoning from the bullet fragment had paralyzed IC1's digestive tract, causing him to starve to death. This was big news: for the first time, they had proof that lead killed wild condors.

Before the discovery of IC1's body, the recovery team still did not know why the condor was heading toward extinction. There were good reasons why this essential piece of information remained elusive. The never-numerous condor ranged widely over impenetrable wilderness. Until the hands-on recovery effort began in 1980, earlier researchers worked alone and with limited resources, making it hard to collect meaningful data. Compounding this problem were Koford's descriptions of a shy and easily disturbed condor, which doomed future studies to onerous restrictions on field research.

When Noel Snyder first began working on the condor program, he read everything he could find about the birds. With his characteristic thoroughness, he then researched related species. Here he came across the record of an Andean condor at the Patuxent Wildlife Research Center in Washington, D.C., that had died after being fed a muskrat carcass containing lead shot. This obscure bit of information leapt off the page at Snyder. He read it again. *Holy shit, if an Andean condor could die from lead poisoning after eating one carcass, might not the same thing be happening to California condors eating hunter-shot game?* Further research turned up a zoo record of two king vultures that had died after eating a lead-tainted carcass. Other studies linked bald eagle deaths with the consumption of waterfowl containing lead shotgun pellets.

In all of the thousands of pages I've read about condors, the words "lead" and "condor" do not appear together until Noel Snyder came along. But even before Snyder set foot in California, he thought lead might be causing the condor's demise. At that point, however, lead was only a theory.

Jan Hamber told me that shortly after meeting Snyder, she and Noel were talking about the condor's problems. "Noel was wondering out loud if lead might be the culprit," she said. "I remember thinking, *That's an interesting idea.* It had never occurred to me."

Similarly, biologist and condor trapper Pete Bloom recalls a recovery team meeting held three weeks after he joined the program. Snyder asked the assembled biologists what they thought was killing the condor. "We rattled off ideas like shooting and egg collecting," Bloom said. "And then Snyder brought up an idea I had never even considered: lead. So, what happens? IC1, the very first bird that we find dead, has a lead bullet in its gut. Pretty amazing."

IC1's death changed everything—and nothing. "We had a sample of one," Snyder said. "It was hardly conclusive proof." Other circumstantial evidence, however, lent credence to the lead poisoning hypothesis. The birds were reproducing normally and food was not a problem; however, condors did suffer from an alarmingly high death rate. Once the recovery team had identified all of the birds, they discovered that *twenty-five percent* of the birds were dying *each year*—clearly an unsustainable number. When Snyder looked at *which* birds were dying, an intriguing pattern emerged. Young and mature birds were succumbing in almost exactly the same numbers, which was highly unusual. Normally, death rates are age related, with many more deaths occurring among inexperienced juvenile birds. Whatever was killing condors was something that even savvy, mature birds could not avoid—such as feeding unknowingly on lead-contaminated carcasses. Adding additional credence to the lead theory were studies showing elevated lead levels in turkey vultures and golden eagles, birds that also ate hunter-shot game.

If lead was a significant issue for condors, then the recovery team had a serious dilemma. Lead was pervasive throughout the condor's huge range, and getting rid of it quickly would be next to impossible. To bolster their case, they needed additional data. More birds needed to die. And more bodies had to be found.

○

In 1984, the recovery team succeeded in gaining permission to collect all first-laid condor eggs. This seeming victory for jump-starting the captive-breeding program actually presented a conundrum for Snyder. If the recovery team took a breeding pair's first egg, the birds almost always produced a second egg later in the year. And if the second egg was taken, sometimes the birds even laid a third; however, because a condor chick depends on its parents for many months, a late-laid replacement egg meant a chick still needed its parents during the following breeding season. In order to care for the chick, parent birds would skip egg-laying, negating the advantage of taking the first egg.

Snyder proposed a compromise: take *all* of the eggs laid by the wild birds, not just the first-laid ones. As soon as a breeding pair had adequate genetic representation in the captive flock, begin early releases of their offspring. Better to impact the wild population in the short term, he argued, in order to ensure a sufficiently diverse captive population.

In late 1984, permission was granted to collect all of the next year's eggs. At the same time, tentative plans were made to release a few captive birds, and several condors were prepared for release. The recovery program seemed to be making good progress. Then the bottom fell out.

The winter of 1984–85 proved catastrophic for the wild birds. But it wasn't until the following spring that the recovery team found out how bad things were. Condors cover great distances, and winter storms make tracking them difficult. When the weather let up and observers began surveying nest sites, they found an eerie emptiness in condor country. Where were the birds? Spotters scoured the mountains and grasslands, but found only single birds at the nest sites — or none at all. By March, five wild condors were confirmed missing and presumed dead. To make matters worse, four out of the five nesting pairs had lost one or both members.

In early April, the recovery team received a worried phone call from a rancher in the Sierra foothills. The foreman's wife had found a sick and debilitated condor near a water trough. The recovery team sprang into action. In the middle of the night, a zoo veterinarian arrived on horseback. Under the glare of flashlights, the vet examined the emaciated and lethargic adult bird. There were no gunshot wounds, broken bones, or injuries, and no obvious reason why it was in such distress. The vet administered an antibiotic injection in case the bird had an undetected infection. From the photo census pictures, recovery team members identified him as Broken Feather. When daylight arrived, Broken Feather grew weaker. All the vet could do was hold the bird's head and watch the life drain from his eyes.

Broken Feather's body was transported back to the zoo for a necropsy. Like IC1 a year earlier, the lab results showed toxic levels of lead. Broken Feather wore no radio tags, so it was great good fortune that they found him at all. The bird's death gave Snyder his second proven case of lead poisoning.

Including Broken Feather, six wild condors were now dead or missing—40 percent of the population. The fate of the other birds that disappeared during the winter of 1984–85 was never determined. A likely hypothesis is that a least some of them perished from lead. Even a single contaminated carcass from which several birds fed could have been lethal. Zoo biologists anticipated collecting as many as thirteen eggs in 1985, but now the only wild condors still breeding were the Santa Barbara pair—the birds Jan Hamber had been watching for a decade. The pair produced two eggs that hatched that year: the total condor egg production for 1985.

The die-off of birds left only nine condors in the wild. Had they passed the point of no return? Snyder feared that they had. Only one option remained: bring in all the birds and do it as soon as possible before any more of them died. Snyder also worried about the lack of genetic diversity among the captive birds. "You face genetic threats when the numbers get too low," he said. They needed the added bloodlines of the wild birds or the species might be doomed no matter what they did. "You're lost long before you get down to the last bird."

Just a few months earlier the program had been going so well that they were ready to release captive birds. Now it seemed madness to put birds back into such a deadly environment.

The proposal to capture all of the remaining birds touched off a furor. It was one thing to take eggs and chicks for captive breeding and quite another to take the last birds. Some opponents questioned if the missing birds were really dead. The National Audubon Society's director of research speculated that the birds had found new nesting areas. But Snyder knew that was about as likely as a condor pair suddenly laying a clutch of a half dozen eggs. Spotters had spent the equivalent of 750 days searching for condors—and had found nothing. The birds were gone.

Taking in the last condors threw the recovery effort into political chaos. The once-recalcitrant California Fish and Game Commission reversed themselves, now voting to *support* the capture of the remaining wild birds, while the National Audubon Society came out *against* capturing the last birds. Audubon was joined by the Sierra Club, Friends of the Earth, and even Snyder's own bosses at the U.S. Fish & Wildlife Service, who took the position that protecting condor habitat was so vital that some birds had to be left in the wild. They reasoned that if there were no birds flying around, wilderness areas would be up for grabs. Dave Phillips, an endangered species specialist with Friends of the Earth, said, "What will this mean to developers who want to put in subdivisions, or to dam builders, oil drillers, and the off-road vehicle people? All these people could rightly say, 'Why should we be restricted when the condors have been sent off to zoos?'"

Phillips had a point. Developers were already eyeing the condor sanctuaries. As Snyder's political support turned shaky, some officials looked at the condor's perilous situation and wondered if the bird was worth saving at all. Why spend more money on a doomed species?

Opponents to capturing the last birds were also concerned that zoo birds were too tame to release, a claim that would prove prescient. They said that wild "guide birds" would be needed to show zoo birds where to nest and forage. If the wild culture of the birds was lost, how would zoo-bred birds know what to do? It may sound strange to talk about the "culture" of the condor, but these very smart and social birds establish long-term relationships with one another, passing along their complex social structure from one generation to the next.

Toward the end of 1985, plans still called for the release of three condors the next spring—unless, of course, the remaining wild birds died. That kind of bizarre reasoning drove Snyder up the wall. He was exhausted from the political maneuvering and the il-logic of an immutable bureaucracy.

"It was all consuming," he told me. "And it was miserable being in the condor program. It makes people start thinking about how they can get out. The truth is, I probably would have never done it if I had known what it would be like. You get eaten up by the things that you know ought to be happening but aren't being done."

"Nineteen eighty-five was the low point?" I asked.

"Definitely. So many birds had died over the previous winter. It was time to bring in the last birds and see if captive breeding would work. That was our only chance."

"But you lost your political support."

"Right. The Audubon Society didn't want to bring in the birds. Even the U.S. Fish & Wildlife Service—my own organization—opposed it. There were still plans to release some birds, but it made no sense. Why throw them out into an environment where they were dying like flies? Releasing birds under those circumstances was committing suicide."

"What did you think could be done?"

"I remember trying to figure out how to get out of the bind we were in. I knew we were going to need some good luck. And I also realized we were not going to win the battle until another bird died."

○

In early November, AC3's radio transmitter failed. AC3 was Jan Hamber's bird, the Santa Barbara female she had been observing since the 1970s. This was the mother bird that had made a sorrowful return to the nest cave, looking for her lost baby after its death at the hands of the recovery team. AC3 is the bird that Jan and I looked at in the Santa Barbara Museum's glass-enclosed display.

Condor trapper Pete Bloom set out to capture AC3 to replace her broken radio. By this time, Bloom was no longer using cannon nets to capture birds. "All the condors had been trapped for radio tagging," he said. "The birds figured out what the cannon net setup looked like from the air. Even though we camouflaged the blind, many of them learned to spot the shape and stay away." So Bloom switched to pit traps.

The beauty of the pit trap is that almost nothing is visible above ground. It is a trench four feet deep, three feet wide, and six feet long. A four-by-eight sheet of plywood is placed over the hole and disguised with dirt and clumps of grass. Bloom would slip in through a "grab hole" cut in the plywood. He positioned an old Pier One Imports wicker basket upside-down over the opening. The basket was camouflaged with twigs and grass and had strategically placed peepholes. Then he would lie and watch and wait.

Bloom was uniquely suited to this work. He had grown up in Southern California, where he developed an early passion for wild animals, especially birds. He trapped his first raptor at age twelve, received his banding license at eighteen, and by the time he joined the condor program, he had trapped ten thousand hawks, owls, and eagles.

"A pit trap is like being in a grave," Bloom said. "It's cold, it's dark, and sometimes there's things crawling around down there.

Not everyone can understand this, but those pit traps were one of the most exciting places on earth. When I sat up in the pit and looked out through the slits in the basket, the birds—ravens, vultures, eagles, and condors—were sometimes six inches from my nose. It was an adrenaline rush."

At dawn on November 23, Bloom arrived at a pit trap for another day's attempt at capturing AC3. He covered the pit's bottom with an old rug and equipped himself with a two-way radio, lunch, a cotton sleeping bag, a book, and a piss bottle. He slipped into the hole and pulled the wicker basket over the opening. Home sweet home.

His support team dragged a calf carcass close to the basket. They pounded metal tent stakes through the animal's neck and rear leg to keep the birds from dragging it away.

One of Bloom's jobs was to collect the carcasses—stillborn calves that came from local dairies. "I'd hose off the dead bodies and take them to a freezer where we stored the calves until we took them to a trap site," he said. "Sometimes I'd have three or four stiff frozen calves with their legs sticking up in the back of my little pickup truck. One time I had a load of calves and I drove through a McDonald's. Got some comments that day!"

Bloom waited in the pit several hours before he received a radio call that AC3 was overhead. He sat up and cautiously looked out through the camouflaged basket. A cloud of flies buzzed over the dead calf, and several ravens picked at it. Soon, Bloom heard the distinctive landing sounds of a condor: a whoosh of feathers brushing against each other followed by a bouncing thud. AC3 pushed aside the ravens and ripped into the calf. She was just inches from the basket covering Bloom's head. A drop of calf's blood flew through the peephole and splattered Bloom's nose. AC3's feathers exuded a faint salty smell, a pleasant odor that reminded Bloom of the ocean. He eyed AC3's legs that looked like two giant drumsticks and waited until both were close. Then he reached up through the grab hole and seized her. Unable to move, she settled on her breast. Bloom held her tight until the support crew ran up. Typical of most

One of the last wild condors sunning himself near his nest site. USFWS/D. CLENDENEN

An adult condor soars over the golden rolling hills of California.
USFWS/A. FUENTES

The first wild-born fledgling from the recovery program (without number tags) with one of his parents. The chick fledged in November 2003 in the Grand Canyon.
© PARISH/THE PEREGRINE FUND

The condor's excellent eyesight helps it to spot carrion from great distances.
© PARISH/THE PEREGRINE FUND

Topa Topa was brought to the Los Angeles Zoo in 1967 as an injured juvenile bird and has resided there ever since. USFWS/LOS ANGELES ZOO

These juvenile birds have dark heads and lack the adult condor's distinctive triangular white patches under the wings. It takes five or six years for a young condor to achieve full adult coloration. USFWS/G. KRAMER

Eben and Ian McMillan were self-taught naturalists who became fierce opponents of the "hands-on" condor recovery program. USFWS

Carl Koford's groundbreaking condor research in the 1940s included visits to nest sites and handling the birds. Later, Koford opposed data-collection efforts and argued that approaching within 500 yards of a nest site could harm the birds. USFWS/E. HARRISON

In an effort to learn more about condor development, on June 28, 1980, condor recovery team members inspected young AC9 in his nest site without incident. Two days later, climber Bill Lehman made a tricky descent down a 75-foot cliff to examine the other known nestling that year called the Santa Barbara chick. The chick died from the stress of being handled, and the resulting uproar over the tragedy nearly ended the condor recovery program.
USFWS (ABOVE); USFWS/J. FOOTT (RIGHT)

A condor named Kaweah goes after a zookeeper. USFWS/M. CLARK/LOS ANGELES ZOO

A male condor courts a female by bowing his head and spreading his wings. SAN DIEGO
ZOOLOGICAL SOCIETY

Adult condors often live for fifty or sixty years and usually stay with the same mate through
many breeding cycles. USFWS/N. SNYDER

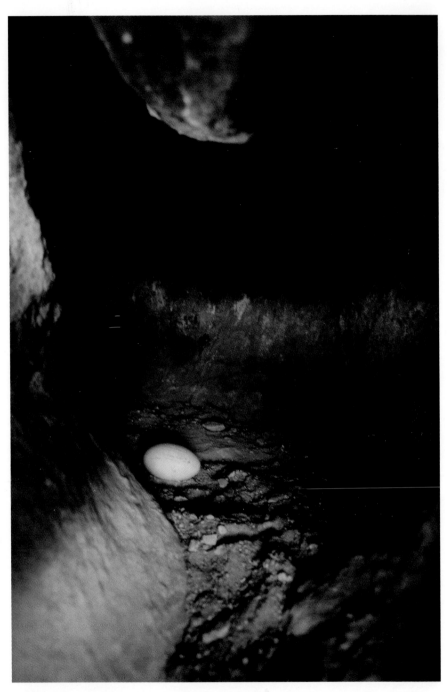

Condors do not build traditional nests. They frequently lay their eggs on the rocky floors of caves found in sandstone cliffs. USFWS/A. MEE

The number tags worn by released condors are visible even when a bird is roosting.
USFWS

Biologists Bill Toone and Noel Snyder made a tricky ascent up a steep mountainside to carry the first condor egg recovered from the wild to a waiting helicopter. USFWS/H. SNYDER

Crews cut makeshift helipads into chaparral-covered hilltops to transport eggs—and in some cases, young condors—from their wild nests to zoos to start a captive-breeding program. USFWS

Biologists used a cushioned carrier box heated with hot water bottles to keep condor eggs safe and at the proper temperature while they were transported to a zoo incubator. USFWS

Noel Snyder helicoptered a number of wild-born condor eggs to zoo incubators to help start a captive-breeding program that was crucial to the survival of the species. USFWS

A zookeeper uses a powerful light to "candle" a condor egg to monitor an unborn chick. USFWS/R. GARRISON

Sisquoc was the first condor chick born in captivity. The egg was taken from a wild condor nest in 1983 and successfully hatched at the San Diego Zoo. USFWS

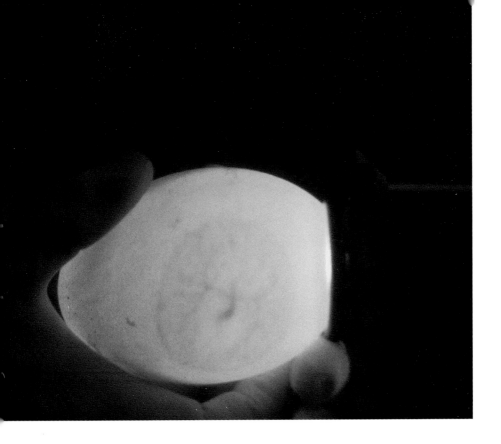

Sisquoc was joined a week later by Tecuya, the second chick hatched in a zoo. ZOOLOGICAL
SOCIETY OF SAN DIEGO

All released condors carry number tags and either GPS or radio transmitters on their wings.
C. PARISH/THE PEREGRINE FUND

Jan Hamber often tracked condors that were equipped with lightweight, wing-mounted radio transmitters. USFWS/S. PETTY

Soaring condors sometimes dangle their legs while flying. USFWS/G. KRAMER

In 1984, a necropsy of the frost-covered body of condor IC1 gave the condor recovery team their first proof that lead bullet fragments from hunter-shot game were killing the birds. USFWS/H. SNYDER

Because ingesting lead from hunter-shot game remains a major threat to released condors, the recovery team provides released birds with still-born calf carcasses.
USFWS/D. CLENDENEN

A golden eagle descends toward a group of condors feeding on a calf carcass put out by the recovery team. USFWS/A. FUENTES

During the 1980s, the recovery team often used cannon nets to capture condors. Blasting caps shot weights out of metal tubes that were attached to the net. The net arced over the feeding birds and trapped them. USFWS/H. SNYDER (ABOVE); USFWS/J. OGDEN (RIGHT)

In 1985, condor trapper Pete Bloom caught AC3 in a pit trap for a routine blood test and to replace a defective radio transmitter. USFWS

Pete Bloom holding AC3. Although regulations required that AC3 be released as soon as the blood test was completed, later test results showed her blood lead level was dangerously high. AC3's agonizing death from lead poisoning led to the capture of all the remaining wild condors. USFWS/D. CLENDENEN

AC8 and AC9 soar together during 1986. The two birds were the last breeding pair of wild condors. USFWS/C. COGAN

AC9 flying over his home range before he was captured. USFWS/C. COGAN

On April 19, 1987, the last wild condor, AC9, was captured with a cannon net on Tejon Ranch. USFWS/ J. McNEELEY

Pete Bloom and Greg Sanders (above) put AC9 into a pet carrier called a sky kennel for transport to the San Diego Wild Animal Park. USFWS/J. HAMBER

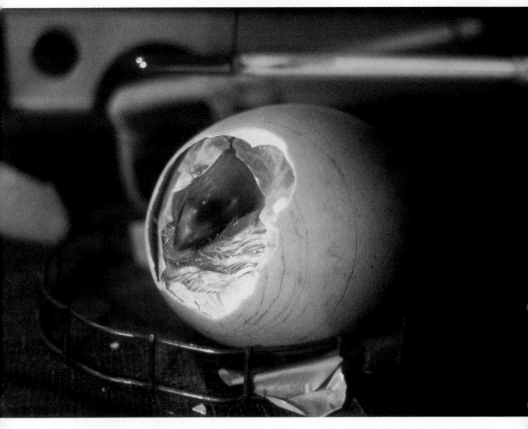

The hatching of Molloko, the first chick born from an egg laid in a zoo, proved that California condors could breed in captivity. SAN DIEGO ZOOLOGICAL SOCIETY

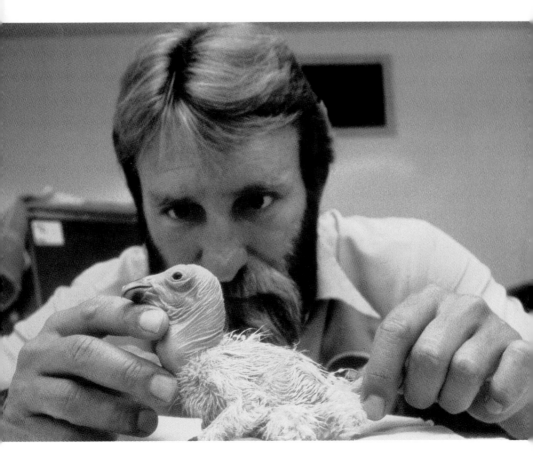

Zookeeper Don Sterner weighs the one-day-old Molloko. USFWS

Zookeepers raise some chicks using handheld condor-like puppets as surrogate parents.
ZOOLOGICAL SOCIETY OF SAN DIEGO

AC8's flight to freedom. In 2000, AC8 was the first of the original wild condors re-released back into the wild. USFWS/FRIER/NIKON, INC.

captured condors, AC3 soon regurgitated a green glop that Bloom says looked exactly like fresh guacamole.

The recovery team replaced AC3's radio transmitter and took a blood sample to check for lead poisoning. "In those days, we sent the blood to a lab for testing," Bloom said. "The rules said that if the bird appeared healthy, it had to be let go, even though we didn't know the lab findings. It wouldn't have harmed the bird to hold it until we knew the results. But the rules didn't allow that, even though we had proof that condors were dying from lead. It was very disturbing."

AC3 looked fine and was released. A few days later, the lab tests came back showing a dangerously high level of lead in her blood. Alarmed, zoo veterinarians recommended her immediate recapture.

Almost at once after her release, AC3 had started to succumb to the lead spreading through her body. She retreated to a labyrinth of sandstone cliffs called Bitter Creek Canyon, and her normal range of three thousand square miles dropped to a quarter mile. Some days her radio-tracking signal barely moved—not a good sign. Pete Bloom, Jesse Grantham, Dave Clendenen, and others tried desperately to recapture her. If they could get her to a zoo in time, veterinarians could clear her system of lead before the damage became fatal.

Because lead poisoning paralyzes the digestive tract, AC3 stopped eating. She avoided the trap-site bait. Recovery team members trekked through the canyon on foot and in trucks in a futile effort to capture the sick bird. Finally, she perched in a tree, just out of reach. If they could only get her down somehow. . . . They brought in a helicopter, and the pilot hovered a few yards over her, forcing her to the ground with the rotor's blast of air. They landed the helicopter nearby, and Bloom ran to catch her, but she had just enough energy to fly out of his reach.

The pursuit went on for more than a month; all the while, AC3 grew weaker. Sometimes her mate would fly in and sit with her, a helpless companion, not knowing why his partner was acting so

strangely. In early January, AC3's radio signal became almost stationary, and Bloom knew she was dying. He mounted yet another
capture attempt. This time, he found AC3 on the ground and walked
up and grabbed her. The emaciated, lethargic bird hardly moved.

"Because her digestive system had shut down, the meat she had
eaten had rotted," Bloom said. "I could smell her from fifteen or
twenty feet away."

Bloom accompanied her to the San Diego Zoo. AC3's stench
filled the helicopter's small cabin; the pilot cracked open the small
sliding window and put his nose to the rushing wind. AC3 was one
sick bird.

The remarkable staff at the San Diego Zoo mounted a round-
the-clock effort to save her. Bill Toone, who had helped Noel Snyder with the first condor egg retrieval three years earlier, was the
zoo's curator of birds. He knew this rescue effort would be a long
shot. Tests confirmed a lethal lead level in AC3's blood, and radiographs showed eight lead fragments in her body. Toone discovered that seven of them were shotgun pellets from an old wound
and definitely not the poisoning source. It was the eighth fragment
of lead lodged in her digestive tract that was killing her.

Lead poisoning destroys the nerves of the intestinal tract's
smooth muscles, paralyzing digestion. Once the nerves are lost,
they do not regenerate. AC3 was starving to death, and there was
little that Toone or any of the zoo veterinarians could do. But that
didn't stop them from trying. The vets flooded AC3's bloodstream
with anti-lead medication and succeeded in dropping her blood-
lead levels. Then they anesthetized her and ran a flexible tube
through her intestinal tract to see if it was blocked. It was not, and
that mostly likely meant permanent nerve damage.

AC3 spent most of the next two weeks in a small, windowless
room kept at a constant 85°F. From behind a one-way mirror, biologists monitored her condition around the clock. AC3 spent much
of her time lying on her side in a bed of straw, growing weaker with
each passing day. They fed her a blend of minced day-old mice and

egg yolk. When that failed, they pumped out her intestinal tract and tried a liquid mixture. That, too, was unsuccessful. Finally, the vets began intravenous feeding, but even that did not work. Desperate, they implanted a tube from AC3's neck to her stomach to bypass her nonresponsive digestive tract. By now, the condor was near death. She could not handle the tube. She pecked at it with her beak and fought to the very end. On January 18, shortly after noon, the light left AC3's eyes.

"The bureaucrats' ruling that we had to release the bird when she was initially captured put us in a horrible position," Toone said. "By the time we recaptured her, she was very far gone. We had to balance letting her die with dignity versus trying everything we could do to keep her alive in order to save the species. There were days of work that we did on AC3 where we knew we weren't going to save her."

AC3 had been one of the family; the loss devastated the recovery team. Toone's voice cracked as he continued softly: "We put a lot of heart into that bird. What happened to AC3 was bullshit. Lead didn't kill her, she died from politics."

○

While AC3 was dying, Noel Snyder became embroiled in further political acrimony. For several months the U.S. Fish & Wildlife Service had argued against bringing in the last wild birds, but AC3's lead poisoning changed their minds. They finally announced plans to capture all the birds.

The decision brought to a head the growing rift between the U.S. Fish & Wildlife Service and the National Audubon Society. Five years earlier, the two organizations had shared a similar goal and approach to saving the condor. Now the alliance crumbled, and they became opponents. Audubon lawyers claimed that it was "biologically unsound" to capture all of the birds. They filed suit in federal district court and succeeded in getting an injunction barring the capture of any more wild condors.

What motivated the National Audubon Society to fight so hard against the capture of the last birds? Since the early 1980s, they had tried to convince the government to purchase Hudson Ranch, a fourteen-thousand-acre expanse of rolling grasslands and oak savannahs in Kern County, California, inhabited by some of the wild condors. With the loss of so much of the wild population over the 1984–85 winter, the Interior Department wavered at spending millions of dollars on a refuge for a bird that might very well be doomed. The National Audubon Society worried that if there were no wild birds, the whole deal would collapse. Eventually, government officials were persuaded that preserving the habitat made sense for condors that would be eventually released from the captive-breeding program. Hudson Ranch did get purchased and became the Bitter Creek National Wildlife Refuge.

"The basis of the Audubon suit was that the U.S. Fish & Wildlife Service had made an arbitrary and capricious decision," Snyder said. "They alleged that there was no new information to warrant the capture of the last birds. That was clearly not the case. The new information—the lead poisoning of AC3—made it urgent to bring in the wild birds. I offered to help the U.S. Fish & Wildlife attorneys in any way that I could. I never heard back from them."

Amazingly, the U.S. Fish & Wildlife Service lost the case. When the ever-meticulous Snyder looked over the court record, he was astonished at what he found. The USFWS was not contending on the issue that they had new information when they decided to bring in the last birds. "Not contend! Why not? They had all the data on AC3's death." Snyder shook his head. "They were throwing the case. The bureaucrats in the middle were on the side of Audubon and did not want to win."

"Why?" I asked.

"They didn't want to lose the condor program. But the case was not yet closed. Fortunately, a USFWS administrator in Washington made an appeal. And on appeal, all the details of AC3's death became public information. Other parties, such as the zoos, furnished 'friend of the court' briefs, and the whole story came out. We won."

Finally, the recovery team had permission to capture the last wild birds. "If AC3 hadn't died, we would have lost the whole shooting match," Snyder said. "From a genetic standpoint, AC3's progeny were already well represented in captivity. If you had to lose a bird, at least her death wasn't critical to the gene pool. Politically, we would never have won the battle without AC3 dying. Tragic as it was, hers was a well-spent death."

○

In a strange twist, as the Audubon lawyers argued in court over the fate of the last birds, the National Audubon Society released a magnificent film called *California Condor*. Robert Redford narrated this prize-winning documentary that, to this day, remains an elegant tribute to the bird. In a sad testimony to how acrimonious things had become, National Audubon Society officials did not attend their own movie's premiere showing. They did not want to be on the same stage with zoo representatives who favored capturing the last birds.

I remember watching the film when it first came out on television. It reminded me of that brief moment when I saw my first condors on Santa Paula Peak. The film left me with a sense of melancholy, and I wondered if it might be the only way I'd ever see a free-flying condor again. Watching it now on video is like traveling back to the 1980s in a time machine. There is a younger Jan Hamber, talking into a radio nearly the size of a shoebox. Noel Snyder retrieves an egg from a nest site in a snowstorm. Pete Bloom fires a cannon net and captures a condor. And there are the birds, flying free. Much of the film focuses on AC3, gliding over the mountains of her Santa Barbara home territory just months before she died.

I never saw AC3 alive. All I have are the stories of those who knew her, this Audubon film, and the glass-enclosed display at the

Santa Barbara Museum of Natural History. She lives there, frozen in time, soaring forever over a molded replica of her mountain domain.

○

The final decision to capture the last birds brought to an end Noel Snyder's active participation in the condor program. Although there were still a handful of birds in the wild, within a year they would be captured and become part of the captive-breeding program upon which the future of the species now depended. There were no more mountains for Snyder to climb, no more of the political machinations that he so detested. Snyder was physically and emotionally drained from the stress of managing a high-profile endangered species program. It was time to move on. In mid-1986, he resigned from the U.S. Fish & Wildlife Service and began work on a reintroduction program for the thick-billed parrot in Arizona.

Snyder's departure marked the end of an era, though his legacy remains. Clearly, one man did not save the species. But Noel Snyder provided crucial leadership at a critical time. In his unrelenting quest to save the bird, he agonized over the details of each decision. He combined brilliant field biology with the audacity to do the right thing, even when it was not politically expedient. Recovery team members speak of his formidable intellect, his unabashed inquisitiveness, and his great intuition. Snyder commanded intense loyalty from many of those who worked for him. When Snyder wanted something done, they did it—no matter what it took to get it accomplished.

○

In 1986, AC9 was still one of the last free-flying condors. The little chick that Noel Snyder and Jan Hamber watched over at his nest site in 1980 survived into adulthood, and his black head and neck gradually took on the exquisite condor rainbow of oranges, pinks, and yellows. Bold white triangular patches developed on the undersides of his wings, and the uncertain flights of his youth became the confident soaring of an adult bird. In December 1984, AC9 was captured, equipped with radio tags, and released. The telemetry data showed that he spent much of his time in the southern Sierra Nevada Mountains, though he roamed widely throughout the condor's range. Once he traveled 115 miles in two hours.

Although he was ready to start looking for a mate, AC9's options were limited in the extreme. Only four other wild condors existed, and three of them were older males. The last free-flying female, a bird known as AC8, had lost her mate in the winter of 1984–85. Despite the advances of the other more experienced males, AC8 took a liking to AC9. In early 1986, the pair began looking at nest sites. They became the last breeding pair of wild condors. AC8 and AC9 lost their first egg, but had a second, which the recovery team successfully retrieved from their nest.

On June 8, 1986, AC8 was taken into permanent captivity. For days after her capture, AC9 searched the lonely canyons for his missing mate. But the skies were now nearly empty of condors. On the very same day that AC8 was captured, the second egg she had laid hatched in the San Diego Zoo. It was the last wild chick ever born.

In December, the recovery team trapped another male. That left just two wild condors: AC9 and AC5. On a late February afternoon, both birds showed up at a trap site on Tejon Ranch. They perched in an oak tree for a while, then AC5 dropped to the ground and began to feed on a bait carcass. Condor trapper Pete Bloom used a cannon net and easily caught AC5. Strangely, the explosions did not scare off AC9; he remained sitting in the oak tree only one hundred feet away. "Whenever we caught a condor in a net, any other birds in the area immediately flew away," Bloom said. "I know it's stretching it a bit, but perhaps AC9 knew he was the last of his kind."

AC9 watched Bloom remove AC5's radio transmitters, place him in a sky kennel, and load the kennel in a truck. Bloom even walked right under the oak tree and looked up at AC9. Still the bird did not move.

When I visit Jan Hamber's office, I always look at her black-and-white photograph of AC9 in that oak tree. He sits silhouetted by the setting sun, watching his only companion being taken away. AC9 spent the last two months of his freedom alone. Condors are social birds. One can only imagine what he must have been thinking: *Where was everyone?*

○

The day before Easter Sunday in April 1987, AC9 circled above a dead calf on Hudson Ranch. He landed, but because a golden eagle was already there on the carcass, he did not feed. Off in the distance stood a woman with a spotting scope. She wore a blue jacket and a Mickey Mouse cap. As the late-afternoon shadows grew longer, AC9 flew to a roost site for the night. The woman followed him in her truck. The next morning, AC9 returned to the dead calf. A few ravens pecked at the carcass, and the woman with the spotting scope again stood in the distance. AC9 warily approached the calf and lowered his head to feed. An explosion ripped the air, and a net landed on top of him. There were pounding footsteps, and human arms pinned him down. Within minutes, AC9 was locked in a sky kennel.

A small group of people gathered around. They stood there for a long time, looking at the sky kennel and talking in low tones. Some of them were crying.

CHAPTER 9

Captive-Breeding Conundrums

ON EASTER SUNDAY, as news of AC9's capture made headlines across the country, activists descended upon the Los Angeles Zoo. They chained themselves to the main gates and graffittied "Free the Condors" on the walls. The zoo's switchboard operators received threatening calls: "We're going to liberate the condors."

Hardline environmental groups such as Earth First! and the Animal Liberation Front had been picketing there for months. Despite AC3's death from lead, they wanted the last condors left in the wild. They also demanded that the zoo release its captive birds. Dave Phillips from Earth Island Institute, one of the protesting groups, urged people to boycott the zoo, saying it was impossible to save the species without a wild population.

Zoo officials had substantial security precautions in place to protect the condor compound. But what the protestors didn't know was that AC9 was not at the Los Angeles Zoo. After his capture, the recovery team had made arrangements with the San Diego Wild Animal Park to temporarily house AC9 there. Later, after the ruckus quieted down, they would transfer AC9 to Los Angeles.

○

Would condors breed in captivity? With AC9's capture, this was the recovery program's number-one question. If the birds did not reproduce, then all the years of effort would have been for naught.

At the San Diego Wild Animal Park, Bill Toone zealously watched over his captive flock for the first signs of breeding behavior. It would have been natural to pair AC9 with AC8, his mate in the wild, but tests showed the birds were genetically too closely related to be mated in captivity. So each was given another partner.

During the early 1980s, Toone had devoted himself to studying other New World vultures, preparing for the time when condors might be brought to the zoo to breed. Even before the recovery team had permission to capture condors, Toone had amassed valuable information about similar bird species. "In those turbulent years after the Santa Barbara chick's 1980 death, I knew if there wasn't a captive-breeding program, there wouldn't be a condor," Toone said. "It was the only way we were going to save the species. We felt we had no choice but to proceed under the assumption that sanity would return, and that we would someday be working with condors. I spent two years studying king vultures, black vultures, and Andean condors. We learned about California condors by proxy. Before we ever had a bird in captivity, we knew how we would handle them."

Toone discovered that the evolution of New World vultures is extremely conservative: there is very little variation in behavior between even the largest and smallest of the family's birds. Because these similar birds were easily bred in captivity, he had great confidence that California condors would do the same.

Nevertheless, in the fall after AC9's capture, it delighted Toone to see one of the males begin classic breeding behavior. The excited condor dropped his head, spread his wings, and rocked his body while circling a female. As weeks passed, the female began responding to the male, rubbing her head and neck against him and nibbling his feathers. The pair also started showing interest in their enclosure's nest box. But the female was not quite ready, and before the male went too far, she would snap her beak at him to send him away. In early February, they finally consummated their relationship. The male stepped onto the female's back and flapped his wings awkwardly to maintain his balance. He held her neck with his beak and folded his tail around hers. It was over in less than a minute.

In early March, the female began preparing for egg laying. She drank lots of water and spent more time in the nest box, rearranging bits of rock and sand. She also roosted with her head and neck in a slightly more horizontal position than normal. On March 4, a beautiful condor egg emerged from her body. Toone had waited eight years for this moment.

Because an older female was paired with a younger, newly matured male, Toone wondered if the egg would be fertile. But when zookeepers "candled" the egg (held a high-intensity light to it), they saw a healthy embryo inside. In order to maximize their chances of success, zookeepers planned to incubate and hatch the egg themselves.

At 6 A.M. on April 24, 1988, the chick pushed its beak into the egg's air pocket. Toone and the zookeepers initiated a round-the-clock vigil. Three days later, the chick pecked a tiny hole in the eggshell. The first rays of light touched its skin.

"We gave the chick seventy-two hours to hatch," Toone said. "If it wasn't out of the egg by then, we planned to intervene." While the chick was fighting its way out of the egg, which now rested on an operating table, she listened to vulture hisses and grunts. These recordings were played in the background in order to mimic the natural environment. Biologists occasionally tapped on the egg to imitate the sound of an adult condor's bill. The hatching went smoothly. At the end of the third day, the chick needed only minor assistance to break out of the last bits of shell. Zookeepers dabbed iodine on the umbilical seal and cleaned her up. By early evening, the newborn bird lay fast asleep in an "isolet," an incubator similar to those used to hold human babies.

Like Sisquoc four years earlier, the baby condor made headlines around the world. This time, however, zookeepers were ready with a name. They christened the newborn Molloko, the Maidu tribe's word for condor.

The next morning, Molloko wolfed down her first meal of minced mice and egg yolk. Within days she was standing on her own and feeding on regurgitated meat collected from a turkey vulture and delivered to her isolet. To keep Molloko from mistaking humans for her parents, zookeepers used a condor-like arm puppet to feed her. They hid behind a curtain and made every effort to minimize human presence.

Molloko soon developed a problem. The isolet's unnaturally hard surface caused her legs to splay out; she couldn't get the traction normally found on a nest cave's sandy floor. Biologists were concerned that her still-soft bones might solidify into a deformed position. To remedy the situation, zookeepers braced Molloko's tiny legs by wrapping them in gauze. Four days later, when the gauze was removed, her bones had hardened into the correct position.

Molloko grew rapidly and within a month had a new home in one of the zoo's flight pens, called "condorminiums," where she could see other condors. By August, she weighed a healthy sixteen pounds and was developing her flight feathers. Molloko had survived to become the first condor ever bred in captivity. And happily, many more followed.

○

Walking across the Los Angeles Zoo's stadium-sized parking lot stirs a raft of long-forgotten memories. I grew up in the Hollywood Hills, less than five miles away, and came here frequently to see the animals and ride the merry-go-round. The chaparral-covered mountains rising to the Griffith Park Observatory are a familiar sight. It is early morning and a flock of Brewer's blackbirds swirl across the asphalt under an overcast sky. The zoo is not open yet, and a maintenance crew cleans the empty pavement with a noisy leaf blower. I'm a long way from condor country.

The entrance resembles a ballpark, with multiple turnstiles and an overhead sign proclaiming in giant block letters: LOS ANGELES

ZOO. Directly to the left of the sign is an even larger painting of a condor, wings stretched wide on a blue background. This is the one animal that greets everyone who enters. It is an interesting choice; the picture is as close as visitors here will get to seeing a real condor. The zoo's captive-breeding program is strictly off limits, though there are future plans for a public condor display.

Today's zoo is quite different from the one of my childhood. I remember a small facility with a display of black bears that I liked. The complex is now vast and modern; it accommodates more than twelve hundred animals. I've arranged to meet Susie Kasielke, the curator of birds, who has been with the zoo since 1979. Susie and I settle in for a cup of coffee at the Safari Café. I ask if she had worried that condors might not breed in captivity.

"We were optimistic because we had a lot of experience breeding Andean condors. There was no reason to think California condors would be any different. It turned out the condor is an exceptionally good breeder in captivity. It's why the population has rebounded so well. With double- or triple-clutching, in two years we can get four to six eggs from a pair that in the wild would have laid only one egg. Roughly ninety percent of the eggs hatch, a phenomenal rate."

Kasielke is quick to caution, however, that despite the success of captive breeding, the species is not yet saved. She mentions several times that rescuing the condor is a long-haul undertaking. It often becomes a lifetime commitment for people who work with the bird.

When I made my zoo visit, more than thirty condors were on-site. The birds had produced eight eggs during the breeding season, with most of them laid in February, March, and April.

"What's it like watching a condor hatch?"

"Very special. I recall early in the captive-breeding program, I was on night watch when a chick was hatching. It was 3 A.M., very quiet, just the soft sounds of the chick breaking through the shell. I was the only person there, watching a baby condor enter the world.

It was a very intimate experience. How many humans have ever had that privilege?" Kasielke brushes back her hair with a rapid hand movement. "It was a magical moment."

Kasielke says that artificial egg incubation requires a lot of skill in getting the parameters just right. "After you work with a species for a while, you can tweak things: change the incubating temperature by half a degree or adjust the humidity a little. We don't try to mimic the variable temperatures and random egg-turning that occur in a nest with parent birds. We try to replicate the *results* that real birds get, not the process."

"Do you provide as much assistance with hatching nowadays as in the early part of the program?" I asked.

"It's really changed. These days, we try to optimize the factors for a successful hatching and do the minimal number of invasive procedures needed, while still ensuring that we get the chick out. But we monitor the hatching process very closely and continue to do so for three days following the birth. We're on twenty-four-hour watch during that critical time, ready to intervene, if necessary," she says.

Kasielke explains that some of the newborn chicks are raised by adults, but since the birds are routinely multiple-clutched, there are always extra chicks without parents. For these chicks, zookeepers do their best to duplicate a natural environment. For the first two or three weeks, the parentless chicks are kept in a small brooder and fed with lifelike condor puppets that resemble a bird's head and neck. A zookeeper will work from behind a black curtain, sliding his or her arm into a puppet and manipulating its mouth.

"We don't want the birds to make any association with humans," Kasielke said. "When we feed the chick with the puppet, the chick is in the light while the keeper remains in the dark behind the curtain. We test to be sure the bird can't see people. We are extremely strict—almost fanatical—about isolating the chick from humans. These birds are sponges for information. Their whole job as scavengers is to learn constantly and to pick up subtleties in behavior. We have to be keenly aware that the chick is looking and listening for every cue. It's a challenge."

"What happens once a chick leaves the brooder?"

"We put them in a more open area that's at room temperature, where they're kept in a tub. We keep using the puppet as a social entity. It appears when the food bowl arrives or when we change the towels. We try to mimic what the parent birds would do. They are strict with their chicks. Chicks that are messing around don't get fed. We want to help chicks learn the social rules."

After two or three weeks in the tub, the chicks are moved to a larger rearing chamber with a screened opening, from which they can view other adult condors. At age five or six months, just about the time they are ready for their first flight, the screen is removed and the young birds can venture out into the enclosure and start to interact with the adults.

These specialized breeding procedures have evolved over time. Early in the captive-breeding program groups of chicks—called crèches—were raised together. The idea was to create social bonds, and it worked all too well. Instead of developing normal condor behavior, where birds are somewhat reserved with one another, the juvenile birds became rambunctious and uninhibited. As we will soon see, these early breeding techniques created problems when the birds were released.

Later in the day, Kasielke and I hop aboard an electric cart and drive up to one of the zoo's two condor compounds, an unimposing collection of portable brown buildings. If it were not for all the chain-link fences and gates, it would look like the overflow classrooms on many school playgrounds. Kasielke introduces me to Debbie Sears, one of the zoo's condor keepers. Sears wears the zoo's uniform—tan pants and shirt; she has worked with the birds for nine years. She tells me that this portable serves as their office and condor monitoring station. Snapshots of recovery team members cover the walls, and condor memorabilia are everywhere: eggs, feathers, number tags, and bones. Several decoy eggs sit on a shelf; these are sometimes used to replace real eggs. I'm skeptical. These ersatz eggs do not look all that much like the real thing to me.

"The birds accept these fake eggs?" I ask.

Sears nods. "They do. There's a biological reason why birds such as condors aren't particular about what egg they sit on. Unlike songbirds, which have to contend with parasitic birds laying eggs in their nest . . ."

"Like cowbirds?"

"That's right. No cowbird in the world has ever tried to replace a condor egg. There's no other parasitic bird that lays an egg even remotely the same size. As long as the fake egg is a reasonable replica, there's no reason for them to think it isn't theirs."

In contrast to the condors' easy acceptance of the counterfeit eggs, they are extraordinarily attuned to the subtlest signs of danger. Sears explains: "Once or twice a year we have to enclose the birds in the feeding area for a while to run some procedures. It's amazing. The one day we actually need them to go into the feeding area, they invariably won't go. They sense something. Even though we do exactly the same thing every day, they know when it's different. We think we must be sending some kind of biological signal. They can't see us, so maybe we're giving off a pheromone they can detect that alerts them to this subtle change."

A bank of computer monitors provides the room's visual focal point. The screens show condors moving about in real time in nearby condorminiums. Sears shows me how she can select from any of fifteen surveillance cameras and bring up the image on one of the larger monitors. A pan-tilt-zoom joystick allows her to obtain any angle she wants.

"These are birds that will soon be released into the wild," Sears says. "Everything is blocked off, and there are visual barriers everywhere, so the birds never see people. We rely on the surveillance system to view everything."

The birds we are looking at are raising their own chicks in an enclosure 30 feet wide, 60 feet long, and 24 feet tall. We watch a male feeding a young bird, the juvenile burying its head in its father's throat. In order to track the birds' growth, old-fashioned spring scales are placed in perch areas. When a bird lands on the scale, a keeper zooms in with a video camera to view its weight. Sears and other keepers also record notes on the birds' behavior as they move about the netted outdoor enclosures. Whenever they want, the birds can also retreat to an indoor nesting and roosting area. The young birds sometimes practice their flying skills by clinging to the enclosure's netting and "net soaring."

A few steps away is another brown portable for birthing condors. Many of the condors that are flying free today entered the world in this place. There's an operating table and an X-ray viewing panel on the wall. The room holds several egg incubators: dark wood cabinets that remind me of 1940s radios. A drum of rotating shelves inside the incubator keeps the eggs at the perfect temperature.

Back in the main portable, I ask about Topa Topa, the male rescued nearly forty years ago and the first condor to be held at the zoo. Sears searches for a moment, and then zooms the camera in on an adult bird. "He's one of our best parent birds. We trust him with everything. It's funny, he's great with the littlest newborn baby, but he hates people. If you walked in there, he'd try to rip your eyes out."

Before I leave, I ask the question with which I always conclude my interviews: "Is there anything else I should know?"

Sears does not miss a beat. "Sometimes writers who only know the bird superficially mistakenly portray the condor as ugly. I hope you'll tell your readers how wonderful they are."

I smile. "That's easy. The condor is a beautiful bird."

◯

In the years following Molloko's birth, the recovery program steadily added chicks to the condor population. By mid-1991, a chick born in the Los Angeles Zoo became the fiftieth California

condor in the world. There was talk that birds might soon be released into the wild.

In some respects, releasing condors just three years into the
captive-breeding program did not make sense. The bird's main
trouble—lead consumption from hunter-shot game—had not been
resolved. But that summer, the scientific panel overseeing the reintroduction effort recommended releasing two condors. They argued that providing clean food for the birds could serve as an
interim solution to the lead issue. Much could be learned, they said,
by having at least a few birds in the wild. They also pointed to gen-
erally positive results from an experimental program that had successfully released a few "test-case" Andean condors into the Sespe
Condor Sanctuary.

It seems more than likely that other factors, too, played a role
in the decision. Having some birds flying free—despite the risks—
would give the recovery effort tremendous forward motion. In the
world of government-funded programs, momentum counts. And it
did not go unnoticed that the Endangered Species Act was coming
up for renewal the following year. A successful condor program
would bolster efforts for strengthening the act.

○

On January 14, 1992, Jan Hamber rose before dawn and prepared
for the day with eager anticipation. In just a few hours, the first
captive-bred condors were scheduled to be released. Ever since the
door closed on AC9's sky kennel, she had been waiting for this moment to arrive.

Jan and her husband left their Santa Barbara home and followed the coastline south for an hour before turning inland toward
the small town of Fillmore. Here they headed into the mountains. At
first light they bounced up the same dirt road that Carl Koford had
hiked half a century earlier. Jan parked near what is now called Koford's Observation Post, at the top of Hopper Mountain. Fog
shrouded the still-dark ridges. Far below, Jan saw a car's headlights

winding their way up the road. Then another car, and another. . . . She watched a procession of headlights glowing in the fog, winding up the mountain to witness the dream of free-flying condors.

Although the release was not open to the public, a long list of recovery team members was invited, as well as reporters and photographers from around the world. Noel Snyder flew in from Arizona, and dozens of other recovery team members—past and present—soon arrived. It was like a class reunion, with people happily exchanging hugs and stories.

In order to get a respite from the gaggle of reporters and cameras, the recovery team scientists were allowed to move to a viewing point a bit closer to the release site. They aimed their spotting scopes across Arundell Canyon toward a clifftop about half a mile away. Shallow caves and cavities pockmark the jumble of sandstone that makes up this historic nesting area where Carl Koford had spent so much time. It was the perfect place to release the captive-bred birds. On most afternoons, gentle breezes waft through the canyon and whorl up the cliff face, providing excellent flying conditions.

Several months prior to the release, the recovery team had built a special flight pen for the young condors at the top of the 150-foot cliff. Constructed from simulated rock, the "cave" opened onto a net-enclosed 30-by-60-foot flight pen. A solar-powered electric fence surrounded the area, deterring predators.

In October, four chicks—two California condors and two Andean condors to keep them company—were flown to their new home by helicopter. They spent the next four months getting accustomed to their surroundings. The California condors were a male, Chocuyens ("valley of the moon") and a female, Xewe ("to cast a shadow"). Each day, observers kept watch with spotting scopes and surveillance cameras. By January, all was ready.

The night before the release, recovery team members removed the net. At 10:31 A.M., the moment Jan had been waiting for arrived. The door to the simulated cave was thrown open, and soon the condors appeared. For the first time in five years, two California condors strode into a world without barriers. The young birds were not accustomed to flying, and no one was quite sure what they would do. At first the birds stayed close to the cave, but within an hour they were wandering beyond the previously fenced perimeter and hopping through the chaparral.

As the freed condors ambled about, Jan thought back to the promise she had made to herself: *One day AC9 will again fly free.* Although the Los Angeles Zoo still held AC9 captive, the release of these two birds was more significant than many realized. The female bird, Xewe, was AC9's daughter.

Bill Toone from the San Diego Wild Animal Park was also present. He watched the birds explore their newfound freedom and recalled the morning nearly a decade earlier when he and Noel Snyder scrambled into a cliffside cave to take the first egg for the captive-breeding program. He remembered the parent bird soaring past the cave opening as he and Snyder removed the egg, dooming the unborn chick to a life in captivity in an effort to save the species. Toone had kept the vow he made to stay with the program until the first birds were released.

"It was the closing of the circle, one that from an emotional standpoint had been open way too long," he said. "And from a biological standpoint, it was the tightest circle you could have spun."

In the early afternoon, Xewe glided about ninety feet to a nearby boulder. Onlookers debated whether that counted as a real flight. Soon the winds turned gusty, and as the afternoon wore on, a Santa Ana gale roared up the canyon. It was a good thing that the condors were staying close to home.

Santa Ana conditions continued through the next day. The media and most of the guests were gone, and the remaining handful of biologists watched with apprehension as powerful winds buffeted the clifftop and tugged at the inexperienced condors' wings. It was unnerving to see the great gusts sweep over the mountains. Yesterday had been a public relations triumph, rivaled only by the birth of Sisquoc. Although program officials had cautioned that the release carried risks, it would be a disaster to lose a condor on only the second day.

At mid-morning, Chocuyens spread his wings just as a gust howled across the clifftop. He rocketed skyward, sailing fifty yards above the cliff. Biologists were terrified that he would be carried out over the canyon and lose control in the turbulent air. Somehow he managed to land on the clifftop. Fortunately, for the rest of the day, the birds stayed put.

○

By summer, the released condors had become more experienced fliers and were ranging farther from their clifftop home. The birds now roosted in places where their ancestors had once perched. But these released birds were different from any condors that had ever flown in the wild. They did not have parent birds to show them the ropes and had not learned to scavenge by themselves. To feed the birds and to prevent them from ingesting lead, biologists put out stillborn calves, sometimes using llamas to transport the carcasses to remote locations.

All seemed to be going well—until July. One day Xewe was roosting on a cliff face about fifteen miles from the release site. She was perched three hundred feet above a creek bed when a group of hikers tromping down a trail spotted the giant black bird. They carried with them a new .22 rifle. Who knows what they were thinking? A shot was fired. Off in the distance, a recovery team observer monitoring Xewe grabbed his binoculars in alarm. Another shot . . . and another. As bullets ricocheted off the cliff, Xewe took wing and escaped unharmed. The recovery team member confronted the shooter, who was eventually convicted and fined.

What is it about big birds that make some people with guns go all stupid? How could anyone hiking in that area *not* know about condors? This was the first time, but not the last, that released condors were shot at. Unfortunately, not all the birds were as lucky as Xewe.

A few months after Xewe's shooting scare, Chocuyen's radio signal went stationary. Biologist Dave Clendenen found his body. He lay face down on a roosting ledge with no obvious sign as to what had gone wrong. Clendenen packed the body in ice and took it to the San Diego Zoo, where puzzled veterinarians did a necropsy. It looked as if the bird had been poisoned, but there was no evidence of lead. A later toxicology report revealed the cause: Chocuyens died from drinking antifreeze. The bird was found near a heavily used camping site. Perhaps someone had left a puddle of coolant there that the bird then drank from—we'll never know.

Despite Chocuyen's death, Xewe was joined in December by six more newly released young condors. Meanwhile, the captive-breeding program continued apace, with "optimism" still the word of the day. Biologists soon noticed, however, that the released birds acted much differently than the original wild condors. The captive-bred birds were not afraid of humans. On the contrary, people and dwellings seemed to attract them. This problem persisted for years, as uninhibited captive-bred birds hung around campsites and buildings. Hikers gave them sandwiches; campers fed them hotdogs. One condor ambled into the office of the exclusive Post Ranch resort south of Carmel. Another perched in a cypress tree in Big Sur over the Esalen Institute's hot tub filled with naked guests.

One day an eighty-three-year-old man heard strange noises coming from his mountain cabin's upstairs bedroom. He investigated and found that eight gigantic black birds had broken through a screen door and were busy shredding his mattress. Carl Koford must have been spinning in his grave at such unthinkable behavior. Clearly, the captive-breeding methods needed modification.

Mike Wallace, who at the time was the curator of birds at the Los Angeles Zoo, remembers the steep learning curve the recovery team faced in trying to rear condors suitable for release. During the late 1980s and early 1990s, cohorts of chicks were raised in a group environment with no older birds present. Without modeling by adult birds, however, the chicks did not learn appropriate behaviors.

"It created a Lord of the Flies syndrome," Wallace said. "It was the blind leading the blind. The birds behaved like a gang of unruly teenagers."

Biologists have learned to keep young chicks in the controlled environment of captivity for a longer time—sometimes as long as two years—to modify the chicks' behavior and better prepare them for release. The early months of a captive-bred chick's life now more closely mimic the condor's natural nesting practices. In the wild, a newborn chick sits alone in a cave and sees primarily adult condors. By using a new approach of raising chicks "singly in a social environment," captive-bred birds are allowed to see an adult "mentor" condor to learn proper behaviors, and they are introduced to peers slowly over time.

Susie Kasielke from the Los Angeles Zoo said, "It's tricky using artificial rearing methods. You have to think one step ahead of the birds—and condors are pretty good thinkers. These early methods of rearing puppet-raised birds tended to desensitize them to new situations and led to uninhibited investigations of things in the wild. They were getting into predicaments that they shouldn't have."

These days, there are disagreements over the best way to raise captive-bred condors. Some biologists remain confident that with more sophisticated rearing methods, puppet-raised birds can achieve success in the wild. Multiple-clutching combined with puppet rearing also offers the advantage of increasing the numbers of condors faster.

Bill Toone disagrees with this approach. "From my experience, chicks are fooled by puppets for the first few days of their life. After that, they want to know what's on the other side of the curtain. It's the Wizard of Oz syndrome. I believe there's nothing you can do about this other than terminate the puppets as early as possible and get the chicks into an enclosure where all they focus on is real condors."

Toone would like to see the recovery program try breeding facilities in the field, where parent-reared chicks fledge their juvenile birds directly into the wild. "Raise them in outdoor enclosures that don't look like human structures," Toone said. "Take the human component completely out of the rearing process. This method has never been tried. I don't believe we know how to raise condors, certainly not like Mother Nature can do it."

Noel Snyder also favors rearing birds in a natural environment. "The problem with condors is that they learn from one another, either good habits or bad habits. If you put out a lot of birds with bad habits, you get bad habits. The birds are now so people-oriented. Part of it is the way they are reared, and part of it is the constant trapping to check for lead, which creates a lot of human interaction."

Snyder notes the difference between today's birds and the original wild population he worked with in the 1980s. He says they never saw wild birds approach people or buildings. He believes that birds who don't grow up around humans won't be attracted to them.

Although the debate on how best to rear birds continues today, back in the early 1990s it was clear to everyone that the bizarre behaviors of the early captive-bred condors presented a significant problem. Then things got worse: the released birds began dying. The first death—Chocuyen's poisoning from antifreeze—seemed like an anomaly; in fact, no other bird has ever died this way. In the spring of 1993, however, a group of released condors began alighting atop power poles. Here was another strange behavior; wild condors almost always avoided such man-made structures.

One day, a bird spread her broad wings and brushed against separate power lines, completing a circuit and sending seventeen-thousand volts of electricity jolting through her body. Two weeks later, another young bird died after flying into a power line. The deaths drained away the early optimism. Biologists discussed moving the birds to the more remote San Rafael Wilderness. At first, plans were put in place to shift the food supply toward this less inhabited area, hoping the birds would follow. Recovery team members even stood on ridgetops flying giant, condor-shaped Mylar kites, hoping to lure the birds toward the more isolated wilderness. But the condors ignored the kites and roamed at will.

Three months later, yet another bird collided with a power line and died. Four of the eight released birds were now dead. Despite having grown the captive population to nearly 80 birds, the death rate among released condors was alarming. Within days, concerned biologists captured the remaining birds with the intent of rereleasing them into a more remote and perhaps safer area. Once again, no condors flew free over North America.

dawn to grab the egg, the male spread his massive wings and hissed and grunted. Wallace took the male's defensiveness as a positive sign of commitment and left the site. Incubating the egg was a good decision; the two parents were taking turns sitting down on the egg. Now Mee wondered if could they manage to hatch their young and launch the chick? As the female thrust her in underneath the male's tail and pushed him away, she then rolled the egg over several times seemingly to position herself. Once she stepped on top of the pale blue egg. The chick was broken; when she last started incubating the egg, her weight crushed the shell.

Out popped the tiny chick. Mee held his breath. The chick looked okay, but the baby bird's sudden appearance confused the inexperienced female. For several hours she struggled to incubate both the chick and the pieces of eggshell. Eventually, she settled down with the chick. Mee was exultant.

The recovery program had come full circle, from the early days when no one knew if condors would even breed in captivity, to this clumsy but successful hatching. For the first time in eighteen years, a condor had been born outside a zoo.

Two weeks after the chick hatched, the male visited one of the area's oil rigs and stuck his head into what looked like a pool of water—instead, it was a puddle of oil. He returned to the nest with his head covered in sticky black gunk, and then preened himself for hours. Mee was fearful that he might have swallowed some oil and would regurgitate it into the chick. He prepared to rush in to help if either bird showed signs of distress. Amazingly, both father and chick survived the oil scare.

A few other released condors in the area were also displaying nesting behavior, and in June, two more pairs had successfully hatched chicks. The three wild-born chicks boosted the recovery team's optimism. Then, in October, just as the chicks were preparing to fledge, something went terribly awry.

Mee found the first chick's body on a ledge below its cave, dead from unknown causes. Within two weeks, the other two chicks had

1 0

A Senseless Death

UTILITY LINE COLLISIONS . . . power pole electrocutions . . . uncondor-like behaviors: Mike Wallace, curator of birds at the Los Angeles Zoo knew something had to be done. Otherwise, how could they possibly sustain a wild condor population?

Wallace decided to attack the power pole problem with a classic behavior-modification strategy that took advantage of the condor's native curiosity and cleverness. He had mock power poles installed in flight pens and wired for electricity. When a bird alighted, it received an uncomfortable but harmless shock. It took only one or two electric jolts for the birds to learn to avoid utility structures. Some birds, seeing their companions avoiding the dummy power poles, never even landed on them.

"Shock therapy" worked. Contingents of birds released after the mid-1990s remembered their flight-pen training, and the number of electrocutions and power-line accidents dropped dramatically. The recovery team also convinced some power companies to bury high-tension lines underground in key condor habitats and to install triangular anti-perching devices on power poles to keep the birds away. It worked so well that to this day, the aversion-training power poles are found at all the release-site flight pens.

At the same time, Wallace and other biologists worked on improving their methods of training condors to avoid humans. They invested more time in preparing young birds for release and made better use of field-based flight pens to ease the transition to the wild. These days, juvenile birds spend several months in such flight-pen "boot camps," learning proper condor behaviors from an older mentor bird and getting acclimated to the area from the safety of the netted enclosure. Once condors are released, the flight pens continue to serve as a home base where the birds can return for food and companionship.

○

The recovery program's newest flight pen is at Pinnacles National Monument, and in December 2003, the *Santa Cruz County Sentinel* asked me to cover Pinnacles's first condor release. I immediately foresaw a problem. Reporters from all over California would be on hand for the condor's return to this historic nesting area. In addition, hundreds of people from the public were also expected to attend. I knew it would be a madhouse: difficult to get interviews, and challenging to make my story unique. My editor and I decided to take a different approach. I arranged to visit the flight pen prior to the release in order to spend an unhurried day observing the birds and talking with biologists.

Two weeks before the release, I drove south on Highway 25 toward Pinnacles. Along the empty two-lane road, I saw vineyards give way to ranches and untamed country. It was a vision of a California from the long-ago past. By the time I turned into Pinnacles, I was driving through a savannah of gray pines and giant oaks.

○

Sheila Foster is waiting for me in her van at the Pinnacles campground. Foster is communications coordinator for the Ventana Wildlife Society, the organization that handles condor releases in Central California. She drives me farther into the park and turns onto a restricted dirt road. Manzanita and coyote-bush branches scratch the sides of the van. Recent rains have turned the road muddy, and more than once our tires spin until they find traction. We follow a narrow valley for more than a mile until we reach a makeshift parking area.

Foster points up the mountain to the flight pen, an unobtrusive wooden building tucked in the lee of the ridge high above us. To get there, we hike more than a mile up a rutted and switchbacked dirt lane. On the way, she recounts the months of backbreaking work that went into building the facility. Condor recovery team members labored in the hot sun, carrying in materials and hammering the structure together.

We arrive at two small outbuildings tucked around a hillock from the main flight pen. "We have to be very quiet now," Foster says. "No noise—whisper only if you have to." The biologists are fastidious about keeping human contact with the birds to an absolute minimum. A footpath circles behind the mountain crest so the birds in the flight pen cannot see our approach. Two or three miles away, a serrated ridge of volcanic spires and cliffs rise out of the Gabilan Mountains. These dramatic rock formations—once part of an ancient volcano that drifted north along the San Andreas Rift Zone—are what gave the Pinnacles its name.

The flight pen's blind is a small wooden building used for observing the birds. It clings to a steep hillside. We approach from the rear and enter a small anteroom. Foster closes the outer door, darkening a windowless transition space. She quietly opens the inner door, and we step into a small observation booth. My head brushes against the low ceiling. Three chairs are positioned in front of one-way glass panes that look out on a forty-by-twenty-five-foot netted enclosure that's about twenty-five feet tall.

In the dim light, biologist Nora Toth looks up from her note-taking and smiles a welcome. She wears gloves and a jacket to ward off the damp chill that seeps through the plywood walls. An exchange student from Hungary, Toth has spent the past year working with the Ventana Wildlife Society to prepare their condors for release. At 5 A.M. this morning she trekked up the mountain by flashlight. She will work until 9 P.M. tonight, recording the birds' every movement and interaction.

I take a seat. Immediately, I count seven condors all perched within a few yards of the one-way glass. Six of them have dark heads: they are the nearly two-year-old juveniles that will soon be released. They all defer to Hoi, a twelve-year-old adult mentor bird whose destiny is to remain in the flight pen. Hoi's job is to teach the younger condors how to behave and interact with one another. Even in the confines of the flight pen, the enormous birds have a regal bearing. One of them hops onto a wooden rail no more than four feet away. Its giant claws encircle the wood; its ivory bill is luminous in the winter light.

Scattered about the flight pen are various perches and a guano-covered scale for measuring the birds' weights. A cement-and-rock water pool built into the pen's sloping dirt floor provides the birds a place to drink and bathe. In one corner stands an electrified mock power pole for their aversion training. A pulley arrangement allows the staff to surreptitiously drag a stillborn calf into the flight pen at night.

To my right, I see a netted airlock-type chamber with two doors built into the mesh. It leads to the outside—and freedom. Joe Burnett, field supervisor for the Ventana Wildlife Society, helped devise this clever system, which allows biologists to select which birds leave the pen—or come back in. It works like this: Bait is placed in the chamber to attract the birds. When a condor begins to feed, biologists use a remote switch to close the inner door and open the outer portal to freedom. To recapture the condors, the system is simply worked in reverse. This is how the birds will be released in the coming days.

Toward noon, Toth and I walk to one of the outbuildings to talk about observing condors. "The birds spend several months here, getting accustomed to the area and learning how to act with the mentor bird," she says. "Each bird has such a distinct personality.

There's a definite social hierarchy, and complex relationships develop among members of the group."

Toth received some disappointing news this morning. The release date has been postponed until the day after her planned return flight to Hungary. "You get very attached," she says. "After all the time I've spent with the birds, I wanted to see them fly. But at the same time, it's not easy to let them go. There are a lot of dangers in the wild, and despite all the precautions we take, there are no guarantees."

Once the birds are freed, biologists hope that they will stay close to the flight pen for safety. They expect that Hoi will act like a magnet to bring them back. So will the calf carcasses placed in a nearby feeding area, which is surrounded by an electric fence to keep away predators. Biologists even hauled a huge dead tree up the mountain and placed the snag near the flight pen as a perch for released birds.

Later in the day, I spend more time in the observation booth. One of the young birds clutches the mesh with its feet, spreads its wings, and "net glides" on the breeze. Another bird lands right in front of my window, and through the plywood walls I hear the rustle of feathers and the scrape of claws. We watch in silence while it folds and refolds its black wings like the robes of a priest.

○

In the late 1990s, just as power-pole aversion training began to achieve positive results, an old nemesis reappeared: several condors died from eating hunter-shot game containing lead bullet fragments. Blood testing on other released birds showed elevated lead levels. It wasn't hard to realize that as free-flying birds ventured farther from their flight pens, they were not always eating from calf carcasses put out by recovery team members. Just as with the original wild birds, consuming tiny pieces of lead proved lethal. Unfortunately, the lead problem has no easy solution; it continues unabated to this day.

It might seem that the condor's lead bullet predicament would be relatively simple to solve: ban these bullets from the bird's range. Unfortunately, instituting a ban involves crossing such tricky political terrain that it has stymied the recovery program for years. Yet unless the recovery team crafts a solution, how will the condor program succeed?

Maintaining the status quo means that some birds will continue to die horrible deaths from lead poisoning and that all released condors will require frequent blood testing. Inevitably, some of these birds will test positive. Those that do will have to go through a chelation treatment in which zookeepers hold them in a small pen and give them twice-daily injections. The medication binds with lead and passes it out through the kidneys. It can take birds days — or weeks — to recover. Sadly, after their rerelease into the wild, some of the chelated birds feed on other contaminated carcasses and require additional treatment. A number of birds have endured multiple rounds of chelation, and two poor birds have each suffered through this process six separate times.

In the long run, the current situation is not sustainable. A condor program that requires regular trapping to monitor lead, constant supplemental feeding, and frequent medical treatment will never achieve its goal of a self-sustaining wild population. In addition, it is unnatural to provision released birds with lead-free calf carcasses — a steady diet of calves from factory farms may not even be healthy. Further, condors are meant to roam great distances in search of food, yet many released birds wait for calf carcasses to arrive rather than searching on their own for carrion. This creates behavior problems and, as we shall see, may even contribute to the trouble these birds are having with breeding in the wild.

○

Ever since the late 1800s, when large numbers of waterfowl died from spent shotgun pellets in Texas and North Carolina, it has been known that lead kills birds. Extensive studies in the mid-twentieth

century showed that ingestion of shotgun pellets was killing millions of ducks, geese, and swans. Some progress in combating the
lead dilemma has been made. Since 1991, it has been illegal for
hunters to use lead shot to kill waterfowl. The ban has brought a
dramatic drop in the number of lead deaths among water birds.

About 80,000 tons of lead are manufactured into bullets and
shotgun shells yearly. Unlike other poisons, such as DDT, lead is
an element and does not break down. Although the health consequences of lead have long been known, humans have often held a
cavalier attitude toward the metal. Lead is useful: it's dense, mal-
leable, cheap, and easily extractable from ore. The Romans used
lead for plumbing—much to their detriment. In fact, the word
"plumbing" comes from the Latin *plumbum* for lead; *plumbism* is the
medical term for lead poisoning.

Lead is extraordinarily toxic to humans: modest amounts can
be lethal. Even tiny quantities can damage the brain and central
nervous system and cause problems with the blood, kidneys,
nerves, and reproductive organs. Low blood-lead concentrations
are known to cause mental retardation in children. There is good
reason why lead has been banned from paint, gasoline, ceramics,
cooking utensils, and plumbing. The only safe level is zero.

O

Grainger Hunt, a senior scientist for the Peregrine Fund, became
intrigued with exactly how condors were poisoned with lead. When
large game animals were shot, the bullets often passed right
through them. If no bullet remained in these animals, how were
condors and other raptors picking up pieces of lead?

Hunt took a hunter-shot mule deer to a local veterinarian and
had the vet radiograph the carcass. He was astonished at what he
saw: a snowstorm of lead fragments filled the X-ray. There were so
many fragments that he had to lay a grid chart over the radiograph
and use a magnifying glass to count them all. Hunt found 472 lead
fragments, many extending well beyond the bullet's path.

Over the next two years, Hunt and his colleagues radiographed thirty-eight hunter-shot deer and found a profoundly disturbing pattern. Nearly every carcass and gutpile they examined contained a cloud of lead particles. Half of the deer samples had more than a hundred fragments and a quarter had more than two hundred fragments. Often the particles spread to a diameter of four or five inches, and if a bullet hit a bone, it scattered even more widely. Some of the deadly particles were as small as fine dust. In addition, some high-velocity rounds are actually designed to virtually explode on impact, leaving a carcass filled with tiny but ever-so-poisonous lead pieces.

Meanwhile, Canadian research with subsistence hunters showed that shotgun pellets ingested from eating wild game were a significant factor in elevated human blood-lead levels. Were hunters using lead bullets running a similar risk?

I talked with Bill Heinrich at the Peregrine Fund, who described a recent study he conducted to examine this question. Heinrich took several deer that had been shot with lead bullets to a number of different butcher shops and had the meat prepared for eating. The packaged venison steaks — exactly what a hunter would take home to cook — were then radiographed. Many of those steaks still contained lead fragments. "I wish hunters knew what they are feeding to their families," Heinrich said. "After seeing those radiographs, I'll never use a lead bullet again."

◯

In biologist Bill Toone's opinion the recovery effort must confront the lead problem now. "You don't recover any species until you address the reasons for their decline. In the condor's case, it's lead. You can't shut up about it. I think every chelation should be a media opportunity to show the public what has to be done to the birds because of lead bullets."

Just as lead poisoning shuts down a condor's digestive system, so have the politics of the lead dilemma paralyzed the recovery effort. The recovery team has had great trouble getting traction on this issue. Thus far, they have tiptoed around the idea of banning lead bullets. Instead, they have reached out to hunters with surveys and education programs. But partial compliance by hunters through voluntary efforts is not enough to rectify the problem. Some bureaucrats in the government agencies affiliated with the condor program are reluctant to confront the gun lobby, arguing that the best approach is to move slowly. But failing to aggressively address the lead problem carries its own risks. How long will the public continue to support a condor program that still has not achieved success?

The recovery program has several possible options for dealing with lead. The simplistic solution—ban shooting in condor areas—will infuriate hunters and is both impractical and unnecessary. Fortunately, new alternative ammunitions that are equal or superior to lead are now available. Solid copper bullets that are virtually fragment free get rave reviews in hunting magazines. An article in the National Rifle Association magazine, *American Hunter*, states that the solid copper Barnes bullets "have met wide acclaim with major ammunition manufacturers and hunters all over the world." Another promising new alternative bullet is crafted from tin, tungsten, and bismuth.

Even the U.S. military has recognized the lead threat and is testing these alternative ammunitions. The military's interest in these new bullet technologies may help raise their acceptance level with the public. These nonlead bullets are somewhat more expensive, but the real impediment to their widespread use by hunters is their lack of availability.

Biologists such as Bill Toone and Noel Snyder think that the recovery program should publicize the human health risks of lead and, at the same time, work with ammunition manufacturers and hunting groups to make nonlead bullets inexpensive and easy to obtain. If necessary, subsidize the cost of alternative ammunition to make it *cheaper* than lead bullets. Or institute a lead tax. However it is accomplished, flood the market with alternative bullets so that a hunter walking into any sporting goods store can easily and cheaply obtain nonlead ammunition.

○

Anthony Prieto was born in 1962 in Santa Paula, near the heart of condor country. As a small child, his grandfather inspired him with stories of the sky giants, and at age four, Prieto saw his first condor in a museum. To his young eyes, the bird looked as if it had a thirty-foot wingspan. The bird made such an impression that Prieto found himself having frequent dreams of soaring condors in deep blue skies. As he grew older, his infatuation with condors continued: he went to the Santa Barbara Museum of Natural History to find out more. Jan Hamber took him under her wing, and Prieto has spent many years volunteering with the condor recovery team, helping to trap and monitor the birds.

Prieto is also a hunter, and that's where he makes his most important contribution. Knowing what lead bullets do to condors, he always felt like a hypocrite when hunting with lead ammunition. In the 1990s, Prieto tried the new all-copper bullets that had just been introduced on the market. He compares the change to the copper bullets to breaking in a new pair of shoes. It takes a little adjustment, but once a hunter becomes used to it, the nonlead ammunition is at least as good as lead. Prieto has proof: he has bagged dozens of pigs and other game using them.

In recent years, Prieto joined with Jan Hamber and two other hunter/biologists to form Project Gutpile, an organization dedicated to educating the public—and especially hunters—about the lead problem and alternative ammunitions. Project Gutpile members give public talks and provide information on lead: the group's website contains a plethora of information.

Each hunting season, Prieto and his comrades hike into the Sierra Madre Mountains near Santa Barbara to speak with hunters about nonlead bullets and to encourage them to bury their gutpiles. Many hunters are unaware of what lead can do to condors—and to them.

These days, the push to solve the lead problem comes from organizations such as Project Gutpile, which are outside the main recovery effort. In 2004, two such environmental groups—the Center for Biological Diversity and the National Resources Defense Council—petitioned the California Fish and Game Commission to ban lead ammunition in the condor range. But when they presented the science to the commission, they ran smack into a political minefield. The commission rejected their proposal, maintaining that "there is no firm evidence that lead ammunition has harmed condors." One wonders what it would take to convince them. Less than two years earlier, a study commissioned by the California Department of Fish and Game concluded that lead ammunition contributes to high lead levels in released condors. The study found that every condor in California had detectable levels of lead in its blood, and nearly two-thirds showed lead levels too high to be considered "background." To anyone familiar with the data, the commission's decision was an obvious brush-off of science in favor of a political agenda.

The commission apparently feared the wrath of a vocal minority of hunters who are set in their ways and suspicious of new ammunition. These hunters claim that alternative bullets don't work as well as lead. Some still don't believe that condors develop lead poisoning from gutpiles. Others don't care at all about condors and tune out the message.

An editorial in the *Los Angeles Times* supporting a lead-bullet ban to help the condor recovery effort provoked angry responses from some of these hunters. Their letters to the editor demonstrate precisely the kind of opposition the recovery team faces. One hunter wrote, "Your editorial advocating banning lead bullets to protect the California Condor is just another backdoor attempt at gun control." Another writer accused the *Times* of writing a "hatchet piece" against hunters and argued that saving the condor was a waste of money.

In any such controversy, not everyone will be convinced. But the data—especially the risks to human health—are persuasive.

Hunting and conservation are not antithetical to one another, and many hunters are eager to help. Indeed, the recovery program would be wise to let hunters lead the way in the transition away from lead.

Sooner or later, toxic lead bullets will be banned. No doubt we will someday look back on this problem the same way we now view lead in house paint. The recovery effort needs bold leadership to pursue the means necessary to make this change. Moreover, the condor team must be deft in making this a win-win situation for hunters and environmentalists alike. Transitioning away from lead ammunition is necessary to protect wildlife and humans.

○

At the start of 2000, an important new chapter in the recovery effort was about to begin. Jan Hamber received news that AC8, the matriarch of the condor program and AC9's former mate in the wild, would be the first of the original wild birds released to freedom.

Jan made a point of attending as many of the condor releases as she could, but every time she saw the zoo-bred birds fly free, she thought of the handful of original birds still held captive. It had been so emotionally wrenching to bring in those last birds, especially AC9, and it filled her with joy to think that AC8 would soon return to the unfettered skies where she belonged.

AC8 had spent fourteen years at the San Diego Wild Animal Park and had produced twenty eggs. But for some reason, for the past two years, she had not been able to breed. Zoo veterinarian Phil Ensley did not know AC8's exact age, but he knew she was an older bird. He brought in a small-animal surgeon, and together they performed exploratory surgery to determine what exactly was wrong. Ensley found that her oviducts were covered in scar tissue, and the damage was irreparable. Her reproductive days were over. Nevertheless, she still had immense value to the recovery program. If she still remembered her old haunts after all her years of captivity, then she represented a thin thread to the original wild condor culture. AC8 was the perfect candidate to become a mentor bird.

In March, AC8 took to the air for the first time in fourteen years—but not under her own power. A helicopter airlifted her to the area north of Fillmore where the first captive-bred condors were released, and biologists placed her in a holding pen. On the day of the release, Jan arose early and drove the dirt road into the mountains. Once again, many of the biologists who had helped save AC8 were there, along with a crowd of reporters. Two immature condors accompanied AC8, and when the door to the holding pen opened and the condors stepped out to freedom, Jan could not believe the difference in the birds. The immatures emerged first, looking confused and hesitant. In contrast, AC8 strode across the clifftop like a queen, her bright-orange head glowing in the sunlight.

No one was sure what the matriarch would do after so many years in captivity. There was talk that AC8 would never recall her old territories. Perhaps she would even fly back to her condorminium at the zoo. Within minutes she took wing, soaring skyward with a graceful pirouette, and sailed across the canyon to a roost snag she had used fifteen years earlier. *She remembered!* Within days she headed for her old haunts in the foothills of the Sierra Nevadas, winging her way 120 miles northward over the rolling ridges and valleys of the old flyway. She had not forgotten a thing.

For the next two-and-a-half years, AC8 ranged more widely than any of the captive-bred condors. As in the old days, she roosted in sites near Glenville in Kern County and foraged for food on the immense landholdings of Tejon Ranch. Often she flew alone. She knew things and acted differently than the captive-bred birds, and they did not follow her.

○

Tejon Ranch is the largest contiguous private landholding in California. The Tejon Ranch Company owns 270,000 acres of grasslands and oak savannahs, an area so vast that it equals forty percent of Rhode Island's total landmass. Much of the ranch remains in its natural state, and for a fee, hunters are allowed to shoot birds, bobcats, deer, black bear, antelope, and other game. Deep in the hills of the ranch lies a small hunting lodge. Half a mile down the dirt road from the lodge is a ravine where hunters dump the gutpiles from their game. At the place where the ravine drops down from the road stands a thirty-foot-tall oak tree: this was one of AC8's favorite roosting spots. AC8 had no way of knowing the dangers lurking in the gutpiles. To her, they were simply an easy meal.

In November 2002, AC8 was found on Tejon Ranch with acute lead poisoning and was rushed to the Los Angeles Zoo. Susie Kasielke, the zoo's curator of birds, told me the story: "It broke my heart to see AC8 brought in. Here was the condor program's mother bird, and she was so sick she couldn't stand. When we tested her blood-lead level, it was the highest we'd ever seen in a condor. In fact, it was beyond high: it was a lead level not compatible with life. We knew we probably couldn't save her, but the keepers mounted an extraordinary effort anyway.

"We radiographed her intestines and found several lead fragments. During the first few days, the keepers went through her feces by hand, and as each lead fragment passed, we matched it with the radiograph to be sure we got them all.

"Twice each day we gave her chelation shots to clear her system of lead. We ran a tube into her stomach to give her food and medicine. And incredibly, she started to get a little better. She even began eating on her own. We never hand-feed wild birds, but we did with AC8. It was all we could do. A month passed, and she continued to fight her way back. It was nothing short of extraordinary that she survived."

Miraculously, AC8 regained her full strength, and two days before Christmas, this toughest of birds was taken back to the Sespe Condor Sanctuary. Jan Hamber and Anthony Prieto had tears in their eyes when AC8 bolted from her sky kennel and soared toward the setting sun. Within days, she returned to her familiar territory on Tejon Ranch, where she continued to perch in her favorite tree.

○

The town of Tehachapi lies one hundred miles north of Los Angeles in a small mountain range that separates the Mojave Desert from the San Joaquin Valley to the north. Britton Cole Lewis, a twenty-nine-year-old cement-plant worker, had spent eight years living in Tehachapi. Lewis was married with a couple of kids, and he loved to hunt.

On a Saturday morning in February 2003, Lewis and his father loaded their gear into a white pickup truck and drove west. The two men were headed for Tejon Ranch. Hunting here is not cheap: it costs $4,000 for a bear hunt, $20,000 to shoot elk. The Lewises had paid $400 to hunt boar in the ranch's "pig-o-rama." These feral pigs can weigh well over two hundred pounds and are a prolific nuisance in many areas of California.

Lewis and his father signed in at the ranch gate and drove the narrow roads that wound through the rain-green hills, looking for their quarry. That morning a dozen other pig hunters, in pairs or small groups, were scattered about the sprawling ranch. Overnight clouds had given way to a crisp winter day, perfect for what hunters call a "ham slam."

By early afternoon Lewis and his father had not yet bagged a pig, and Brit was growing impatient. They drove slowly along a dirt road with a grass-covered hill on the right. The pair rounded a corner and saw just ahead of them an oak tree standing at the side of the road with a ravine below it. In the top of the tree, Lewis spied a large black bird.

"Look," he said. "A buzzard!"

Hearing the truck, AC8 turned her head and looked toward the hunters. Seeing people here was not unusual. AC8 was used to occasional cars and trucks passing by on their way to the nearby hunting lodge.

Lewis jammed on the brakes and grabbed his Ruger 7-mm high-powered hunting rifle. He hopped out of the truck and rested his gun on the open driver's door. Lewis fixed AC8 in the crosshairs of his Leupold scope. Although the bird was a couple of hundred feet away, the powerful scope showed every detail of AC8's enormous black body and orange head. The large blue number tag attached to her wing glinted in the sun. Her red eyes were looking straight at him. A breeze stirred the oak leaves, their pale undersides shimmering. The air smelled of spring grass.

Britton Cole Lewis squeezed the trigger.

The report echoed off the hills and rolled down the canyon. AC8 crumpled into the treetop, the branches cradling her body.

11

AC8's Day in Court

MARK HALL WAS worried. Hall managed the Hopper Mountain
National Wildlife Refuge, and over the weekend he noticed that the
tracking signal from AC8's wing-mounted transmitter had taken a
nosedive. During the winter, it was not unusual for a bird to stay
put for a while, but AC8's satellite transmissions showed no movement at all. By Monday, as the satellite hits stubbornly refused to
move, Hall knew that they had a problem.

Monday night a powerful winter storm roared through Southern California. Despite the weather, Hall was determined to get to
the bird the next day. By midday Tuesday, the downpour had let up
enough for him to drive the rain-slick roads from his Ventura office
to AC8's still-motionless signal on Tejon Ranch. His mood matched
the dismal weather: he knew what awaited him.

Hall had called ahead to the ranch to ask for help in navigating
the network of remote roads. Hunting guide Cody Plank met Hall,
and the two men drove into the cloud-covered mountains. Hall
used his portable radio-tracking receiver to guide them toward
AC8. The overcast sky and wreaths of fog made for poor visibility.
Hall and Plank bumped and lurched their way up several miles of
dirt road until the *beep, beep, beep* of the radio signals grew insistent.
Hall stopped his SUV and peered into the gloom. Ahead was the
mist-shrouded silhouette of an oak tree at the side of the road. Hall
walked almost to the tree's base before he spotted a dark phantom

suspended in the top branches. The wings were splayed out in an unnatural position.

Although Hall had prepared himself for this, it was nevertheless a shock to see AC8's body. Now he had to figure out how to retrieve her. Cody Plank offered to climb the tree. He pulled himself into the branches and scaled his way up high enough to shake the bird loose. AC8 tail-dived into the muddy earth, making her final landing in a black-feathered cascade.

A nasty wound stretched across the old bird's chest. It appeared as if she had been shot, but a necropsy would be needed to confirm it. Hall searched the area: no tire tracks, no footprints, no shell casings. Nothing. He placed the body in an ice chest and started the long drive back to Ventura. The clouds were lowering, and it began to drizzle again.

○

While Mark Hall was on his way to find AC8, Jan Hamber was having lunch with Anthony Prieto, the young hunter who was active with Project Gutpile. They talked about AC8's recent back-from-the-dead recovery and how gratifying it was that she once again flew free. When they parted, neither of them had an inkling of her fate.

Late in the afternoon, Jan received an urgent call from Anthony. The terrible news left her speechless. A long, sorrowful silence filled the phone line. Jan thought of the risks so many people had taken to protect AC8, and of all the years the bird had spent caged in a zoo condorminium. She recalled AC8's glorious release two years ago and how the Los Angeles Zoo's keepers had put their hearts and souls into saving her from lead poisoning. To have it all blown away in one thoughtless moment was incomprehensible. Of all the ways to lose a bird, this was beyond tragic. It was simply stupid.

The recovery team reacted to AC8's killing with grief and anger. And the magnitude of the loss touched thousands of others who never knew AC8 but still cherished what she represented.

Even the governor of California expressed his outrage at such a senseless death. Meanwhile, several conservation groups pledged more than $30,000 in reward money to find the culprit. *Who would have done such a thing?*

○

Veteran U.S. Fish & Wildlife special agent Brett Dickerson walked in circles around the oak tree where AC8 was shot. Like Mark Hall, he could find no evidence pointing to AC8's killer. Dickerson had been assigned to lead the investigation into AC8's death and had immediately driven to Tejon Ranch to search for clues. After his unsuccessful preliminary visit, he brought in a crew of agents and lab technicians to spend a morning painstakingly combing the area and reconstructing the crime scene. They, too, came up empty-handed.

Meanwhile, Dickerson received the necropsy results from the U.S. Fish & Wildlife Service forensics lab, confirming that AC8 had been shot with a high-powered rifle. The bullet blew through the bird and exited through one of her wing tags. She never had a chance.

On the one hand, Dickerson and his team had been lucky that AC8's body had caught in the tree. Had she fallen to the ground, her killer most likely would have disposed of the corpse and her death would have forever remained a mystery. Nevertheless, they still had no evidence and no leads. Dickerson's last best hope lay with the hunters who were on Tejon Ranch the day of AC8's shooting. One of them was almost certainly the killer—but *which* one? The ranch kept careful records. Only a dozen people had permission to be hunting that weekend. Dickerson obtained their names and dispatched his agents to start questioning them.

The first interviews turned up nothing. The hunters tried to be helpful, but no one had seen or heard anything. One of the hunters did mention that a father-and-son team might have been shooting at birds. It was the only lead they had. Their name was Lewis.

When two of Dickerson's agents arrived at Britton Cole Lewis's home, Lewis was cooperative and calm. Yes, he had gone pig hunting with his father on Tejon Ranch that weekend, but he didn't know anything about a dead condor. Lewis was very convincing. It looked like another dead end.

While the two agents were questioning Brit Lewis, Dickerson visited Lewis's father, Richard, at the plant where he worked. The two sat down at a conference table in the plant manager's office, and Dickerson asked the elder Lewis about the pig hunt.

Richard Lewis described the hunting trip with his son, but denied that they had anything to do with AC8's death. Dickerson told him, "Some people are saying a father-and-son team was shooting at birds." Richard Lewis replied, "Well, the reason they might have thought we were shooting at birds is that Brit was sighting in on some crows. That's all he was doing." The story rolled right off Richard Lewis's tongue. Dickerson was skeptical. He told Lewis how important AC8 was, appealing to the older man to do the right thing and disclose anything he knew. But Richard Lewis stuck by his story.

Dickerson was running out of questions when his cell phone rang. It was the one of the agents at Brit Lewis's house, calling to see what Dickerson had learned. Richard Lewis listened in on Dickerson's side of the phone conversation with growing alarm, receiving the impression that Brit had confessed. When Dickerson hung up, Richard slumped forward and said, "Okay. Here's what happened."

○

Back at Brit Lewis's place, the two agents questioning Lewis were still listening to him proclaim his innocence when Dickerson phoned them back.

"Brit Lewis is our man."

Confronted with his father's confession, Lewis's denials crumbled. Although he admitted to shooting AC8, Lewis insisted that he thought he had shot a turkey vulture. The distinction would prove crucial when it came to prosecuting Lewis under the Endangered Species Act.

Lewis cooperated with the agents and led them to the rifle that killed AC8. He had dismantled the weapon and stashed its parts in different places. In searching the house, agents also discovered the mounted head of a white-tailed deer that Lewis had poached in Illinois. Lewis would now face even greater legal troubles.

○

Look no further than the Endangered Species Act for the single most important legal bulwark safeguarding endangered species and preserving the biodiversity of important habitats. It was the ESA that obligated the U.S. Fish & Wildlife Service to fund the hands-on condor management effort of the 1980s. Without the ESA, there would almost surely be no California condors today.

This landmark act protects more than twelve hundred threatened and endangered species in the United States. Written in 1973, the ESA was one of many major environmental laws enacted during the 1970s, a decade marked by an increased awareness that rapid population growth, habitat loss, and the unsustainable exploitation of natural resources were taking a terrible toll on our planet.

In contrast to the partisanship that divides Washington today, the ESA sailed through Congress with unanimous support in the Senate and only four dissenting votes in the House. With great fanfare, President Nixon signed it into law.

Legislators designed the ESA to begin reversing centuries of environmental destruction and to secure the health of our nation's ecosystems. The ESA empowers the government to identify a species threatened with extinction, formulate a recovery plan, and preserve critical habitat for that species' survival. The condor recovery program is a classic example of the ESA in action.

Along with the condor, the ESA has been instrumental in saving other species, among them, the gray wolf, the peregrine falcon, the sea otter, the whooping crane, the black-footed ferret, the brown pelican, the American alligator, the gray whale, and the bald eagle, our national bird. In addition, the ESA also makes it illegal to kill listed species—or, at least, it used to. Recent changes have weakened many parts of the ESA, including this one.

Although the ESA is not perfect, it is based on the scientific understanding that each species in a healthy ecosystem plays a role in sustaining our planet's web of life. Removing a species frays this web and can set in motion a cascade of unforeseen consequences. Senator Harrison Williams, who managed the ESA's passage in the Senate, spoke of the fundamental principle behind the act: "Each species is a part of an immensely complicated ecological organization, the stability of which rests on the health of its components." Species loss is irreversible, and the only solution is prevention. The ESA enshrines this principle into law. Perhaps just as important as saving individual species, the ESA promulgates the idea that wildlife must be saved and that the government should play an important role in that effort.

○

While the ESA was not without critics and controversy, it remained largely intact until the year 2000, when the George W. Bush administration took office. Since then, Bush appointees have systematically worked to weaken the ESA. They have dragged their feet in enforcing the act, ignored court-ordered deadlines, and greatly underfunded its budget. The administration has fiercely resisted adding any new species to the list that receives ESA protection. During the elder Bush's administration, an average of fifty-eight species was listed annually; during the Clinton years, it was sixty-five. George W. Bush's administration has averaged a paltry *eight*, by far the lowest number of any president. During his term, there has yet to be a voluntary listing; all the additions have been court-ordered. The administration even tried to persuade Congress to eliminate a citizen's right to petition for a listing. Fortunately, Congress had the good sense to refuse.

Some Bush appointees do not believe in the ESA. Craig Manson, who spent four years as Bush's assistant secretary of the Interior for Fish, Wildlife, and Parks, oversaw the U.S. Fish & Wildlife Service, a lead agency in protecting species on the brink of extinction—such as the California condor. Manson went so far as to assert that preserving species was not necessarily the right course. He said, "If we are saying that the loss of species in and of itself is inherently bad—I don't think we know enough about how the world works to say that." This flies in the face of basic ecology theory, which measures an ecosystem's health by its complexity and species diversity. Manson and other Bush appointees want to do away with the act's regulatory functions and depend instead on voluntary cooperative partnerships and incentives.

In 2005, the administration supported efforts to rewrite the ESA, making it more difficult to list species and, perhaps even more detrimental, harder to set aside habitat for them to recover in. Currently, only a third of the ESA-listed species have critical habitats designated for them. The Bush administration seems more interested in opening protected habitats to new development than in conserving resources for future generations.

The administration's drive to open public lands to loggers, oil drillers, miners, and developers extends right into condor country. In 2005, despite strong public protests—including nearly eight thousand letters written in opposition to the decision—the U.S. Forest Service opened 52,000 acres of California's Los Padres National Forest to oil and gas exploration. The decision allows oil drilling right up to the boundary of the Sespe Condor Sanctuary. Opponents decried the desecration of this spectacular and pristine wilderness area. They argued that condors use the entire forest as feeding grounds, and that increased development will harm the recovery effort. Drilling near condor nesting areas already creates an unnatural human presence. Birds have ingested trash left around the oil rigs and have even been covered in oil.

So, how much oil is estimated to lie under the newly opened forest land? Less than the United States uses in one day.

◯

Since condors are protected under the ESA, Britton Cole Lewis's penalties for killing AC8 could have included up to a year in prison and a $100,000 fine. But Bob Wright, the assistant U.S. attorney assigned to prosecute the case against Lewis, had a problem. A little-known 1998 Justice Department policy changed how ESA violators could be prosecuted. The policy stemmed from an incident in Montana where a man who killed a wolf near Yellowstone National Park claimed that he had mistaken the animal for a wild dog. Prior to enacting this policy, prosecutors who showed that a suspect had killed an endangered species could ask for a conviction. Under the new Justice Department policy, Bob Wright had to prove that Lewis *knew* he was killing a condor. Lewis, of course, had claimed that he thought he'd shot a turkey vulture.

Who can say what someone was thinking? Unless a suspect confesses to knowingly killing an endangered animal, it is now almost impossible to get a conviction under the ESA. Instead, a suspect must be prosecuted under other state and federal laws, which typically carry lighter penalties. The loophole allows killers of our country's most imperiled species to escape ESA prosecution. The policy also departs from the conventional understanding that ignorance of the law is not an excuse. A person driving down the highway at ninety miles an hour cannot avoid a ticket by claiming that he or she did not see the speed-limit sign. But shoot a condor? All one has to do is claim that it looked like a buzzard—as Britton Cole Lewis did—and prosecution under the ESA can be evaded.

When attorney Wright found his case stymied by the Justice Department policy, he asked the solicitor general's office in Washington, D.C., to reconsider. He believed that Lewis's deliberate killing of AC8 merited prosecution under the Endangered Species Act. But several weeks of negotiations failed to produce a change.

Washington bureaucrats arguing in favor of the new policy offered the hypothetical example of a rancher who drained a pond, and in doing so killed an endangered species of frog, thus becoming liable for prosecution. Wright disagreed. There was a difference between an accident and an intentional act.

When the Bush administration refused to budge, Wright was forced to file charges against Lewis under the Migratory Bird Treaty Act, a statute that carries lesser penalties. Britton Cole Lewis dodged a bullet.

Wright also charged Lewis with illegally transporting to California the mounted head of the white-tailed deer he had poached in Illinois. Ironically, poaching the deer and carrying it across a state line carried a greater potential penalty than killing AC8.

○

At Lewis's May 14, 2003, arraignment in federal court, his attorney immediately went on the offensive. Instead of a guilty plea, he asked the judge to allow Lewis to plead *nolo contendere* ("no contest") to both counts against him. It was an important difference, and Wright vigorously objected. He pointed out that a no-contest plea meant that Lewis only admitted guilt in order for the court to impose punishment. For all other purposes, Lewis was, in effect, denying any wrongdoing. Wright argued that allowing this plea minimized the seriousness of the offense, made it look as if the government had a weak case, and did not serve as a deterrent to others.

Faced with the government's objections, Lewis's attorney backed down, and Lewis pled guilty to both counts. The whole matter took less than half an hour, and sentencing was set for August at the federal building in Fresno.

○

August in Fresno is relentlessly hot. Fresno also ranks as the nation's second smoggiest city: a pallid haze clings to the horizon. Almost two years to the day after Lewis's sentencing, I drive through

Fresno's outskirts, passing cheap motels and the remnants of old orchards. A flashing bank sign reads 10:33 A.M., 102°F. I'm headed for the B. F. Sisk Federal Building, a five-story cement fortresslike structure that dominates the city's downtown. The many electronic transmission towers sprouting from its roof make it resemble a battleship. Ungainly metal grills shield the windows. On the wall next to the entrance hangs a replica of the Great Seal of the United States bearing the words *Annuit Cœptis*: "Providence favors our undertakings." I wonder if that includes the condor.

Inside, the air conditioning is heavenly. After presenting my identification and passing through a metal detector, I head for the fifth floor to research the Lewis case. The hallway's polished stone veneer walls do little to soften the building's bunkerlike architecture. Guards are everywhere.

After a couple of hours, I take a break and wander down to the third floor to see Courtroom 4, the chamber where Lewis was sentenced. I peer through a small window in the locked door but can see nothing of the darkened courtroom. A guard eyes me suspiciously, and I feel awkward about leaving without an explanation. I walk over and chat with him for a minute. He is a retired game warden and is interested in condors. After a few minutes of conversation, he unlocks the courtroom door and turns on the lights. A pattern of large gray squares covers the walls, and boxy light fixtures hang from the ceiling. It is here, in this claustrophobic room, that Britton Cole Lewis would receive his sentence.

○

On the morning of August 15, 2003, Jan Hamber arrived at the federal building in Fresno and rode the elevator to Courtroom 4. Jan and a dozen other supporters had come to bear witness to AC8's life. Although Jan would not be allowed to speak at the sentencing, she wanted Lewis to see the faces of some of the people who had struggled so hard to save AC8. She wore a T-shirt made especially for the occasion with a picture of AC8 on the front and this inscription on the back:

AC8 Forever Free

In order to leave a legacy,
You have to live a legacy.

Jan and her group sat in the four rows of pewlike benches at the back of the courtroom, while Lewis huddled with his attorney at a table in front of the judge's bench. Lewis dressed neatly for the sentencing and had cut his dirty-blond hair short. He leaned back in the leather chair and avoided looking at Jan's group. It gave Jan the chills to think that the clean-cut, humble-appearing young man in front of her could have done what he had done.

The U.S. magistrate judge entered and called the case of the United States of America versus Britton Cole Lewis. Attorney Wright began by outlining the charges against Lewis:

"Your Honor," he said, "this matter has huge public importance. The condor was a matriarch of the breeding program. The loss was a tragic one. It was a senseless tragedy."

Wright described how Lewis shot AC8. He noted that Tejon Ranch gave to all hunters on the property a pamphlet with the clear warning: "Don't shoot large birds, it might be a condor. This is a California Condor area." He recounted Lewis's cover-up of the crime, including lying to investigators and hiding his rifle. The U.S. Fish & Wildlife Service estimated AC8's value at $179,998, Wright said. He concluded by stating that his office would accept the recommendations of the probation report.

Jan leaned forward to hear Lewis's fate as Wright read the sentence agreed upon by the attorneys. For both shooting AC8 and poaching the white-tailed deer, Lewis received five years' probation, two hundred hours of community service, and a $20,000 fine.

In addition, he had to forfeit his rifle and was not allowed to hunt for five years.

Jan exchanged a discouraged look with some of the other supporters. They had hoped for a greater punishment—at least a thirty-day jail sentence—to send a message that shooting condors carried serious consequences.

Lewis's attorney addressed the court: "Your Honor, I do want to say on behalf of Mr. Lewis that he is fully aware of the magnitude of what he did. He does hope with his community service time, that he can make others aware of his errors so that hopefully they won't make the same mistake he did. I've contacted the Sierra Club, the California Conservation Corps, and just about every other organization to see whether they have some program they can have him doing . . ."

Jan imagined what she would like to see Lewis do for his community service: *I want him to collect stillborn calves from the dairies and carry them to Hopper Mountain. I want him to get up at 4 A.M. to put out the carcasses, then sit in a blind all day under a broiling sun and keep track of which birds come to feed. I want him to learn how hard people are working to bring back this species.*

At the end of the sentencing, Britton Cole Lewis spoke directly to the judge. He asked forgiveness for shooting AC8 and talked about the grief his actions had brought to his family. He denied that he received the information from Tejon Ranch that there were condors in the area. He concluded his remarks by saying: "Being an avid hunter, I can honestly say I knew nothing about the condors. I knew nothing about these birds. And I believe that I should be punished for my actions. There's no doubt. And that's all."

Lewis's attorney mentioned again the importance of performing community service so that Lewis's mistake would be heeded by others. The sentencing ended, and Lewis hurried from the courtroom, head down, eyes averted. He did not want to talk with the condor people.

Afterward, reporters asked Jan for her reaction:

"I'm not antihunter," she said. "But if someone has paid to go out and shoot pigs, you'd expect them to know that the pig isn't going to be sitting in the top of a tree. AC8 was a very important bird. There were thousands of hours put into saving her. It's a joke to say she was only worth about $180,000. You can't put a price on this kind of loss." She shook her head. "I don't understand why someone would do something like this. I just don't understand . . ."

AC8's supporters took a group photo in front of the federal building, gathering around a massive, waist-high cement planter box that doubled as a barricade. Jan stood in the back row, trying to smile. In the photo, her AC8 T-shirt is barely visible.

○

Many in the condor program reacted with bitter disappointment to Lewis's misdemeanor conviction. In the words of Peter Galvin, California and Pacific Director of the Center for Biological Diversity, "This weak enforcement action is an outrage to anyone who cares about protecting our legacy for future generations. The slap-on-the-wrist charges filed by the Bush Administration in this case once again clearly show their complete lack of commitment to protect America's endangered wildlife and national heritage. The charges filed in this case are a disgrace to the office of Attorney General, to the memory of AC8, and to the condor recovery program as a whole."

After Lewis paid his fine, one more court action followed. Despite Lewis's earnest assurances about the importance of performing community service, a few months later he told his probation officer that he was too busy to complete his two-hundred-hour commitment. The court agreed to waive his community service obligation and allowed him to buy his way out. They calculated the amount by multiplying the two hundred hours by the minimum wage. Instead of educating others about his mistake, Lewis simply paid an additional $1,350.

12

Shadows in the Sky

TROUBLE STARTED AS soon as the female condor entered the nest cave. She wanted to begin her incubation duties, but the male, who was sitting on their egg, did not move. In the dim light, the female glared at her mate with beady-eyed concentration. Neither bird gave ground.

Biologist Allan Mee had discovered their nest in a remote canyon in the Ventura County backcountry in February 2002. For the past two months, he had spent much of his time bent over a spotting scope, watching these newly adult birds make a nesting attempt. Although the birds had been released a few years earlier, they had only recently become sexually mature. Usually a confrontation between the birds would not have overly concerned him, but theirs was no ordinary egg. This condor pair was within days — perhaps hours — of being the first captive-bred birds to successfully hatch an egg in the wild. This morning Mee noted a crack snaking its way across the eggshell. It looked as if the chick had already started to hatch. The parent birds had picked a terrible time for a domestic squabble.

Mee had had early doubts about the male's nesting ability. The father bird seemed uninterested in incubating the egg; he left the female alone for days at a time. So Mee made plans to remove the egg and take it to the Los Angeles Zoo for hatching. But when biologist Mike Wallace rappelled down a seventy-five-foot cliff to the nest cave to grab the egg, the male spread his massive wings and hissed and grunted. Wallace took the male's defensiveness as a positive sign of commitment and left the egg in the nest. It was a good decision: the new parents went on to successfully incubate the egg. Now, Mee wondered, could they manage to finish their job and hatch the chick?

The female thrust her head under the male's tail and pushed him away. She turned the cracked egg over several times, seemingly oblivious to the broken shell. She even stepped on top of the pale blue orb. The crack widened, and when she at last started incubating the egg, her weight crushed the shell.

Out popped the tiny chick. Mee held his breath. The chick looked okay, but the baby bird's sudden appearance confused the inexperienced female. For several hours she struggled to incubate both the chick and the pieces of eggshell. Eventually, she settled down with the chick. Mee was exultant.

The recovery program had come full circle, from the early days when no one knew if condors would even breed in captivity, to this clumsy but successful hatching. For the first time in eighteen years, a condor had been born outside a zoo.

Two weeks after the chick hatched, the male visited one of the area's oil rigs and stuck his head into what looked like a pool of water—instead, it was a puddle of oil. He returned to the nest with his head covered in sticky black gunk, and then preened himself for hours. Mee was fearful that he might have swallowed some oil and would regurgitate it into the chick. He prepared to rush in to help if either bird showed signs of distress. Amazingly, both father and chick survived the oil scare.

A few other released condors in the area were also displaying nesting behavior, and by June, two more pairs had successfully hatched chicks. The three wild-born chicks boosted the recovery team's optimism. Then, in October, just as the chicks were preparing to fledge, something went terribly awry.

Mee found the first chick's body on a ledge below its cave, dead from unknown causes. Within two weeks, the other two chicks had also perished. A necropsy on one of the birds turned up a startling discovery. Its stomach bulged with a virtual junkyard of trash: twelve bottle caps, shards of glass, wiring, screws, and washers. More trash littered the chick's nest cave. Zinc absorbed from the washers had poisoned the bird.

In the following year, one chick had to be euthanized after glass shards perforated its stomach and caused respiratory damage. Another chick who had been taken to the Los Angeles Zoo with a broken wing had almost a pound of trash in its stomach, including thirty-five bottle caps. As time passed, more wild-born chicks in Southern California died, many of them from ingesting so much "microtrash" that their digestive tracts were blocked.

The good news is that released condors have pretty much matched the hatching rate found in the original wild population; however, fledging success has been poor, with much of the failure due to microtrash. The issue of microtrash has become a persistent and lethal problem. Released condors feed their chicks all sorts of junk. Everything from pieces of car taillights to bullet-shell casings have been removed from the digestive tracts of wild-born chicks. There has been much speculation about the causes of this problem and possible solutions to it.

Adult condors are hardwired with an instinctual behavior to seek out small, hard objects. The search image is general enough so that condors do not differentiate between a bone chip and a piece of metal or plastic. Some biologists speculate that the birds are looking for bone fragments to provide calcium for their chicks. Others theorize that the small objects are used to create a mass to help the birds regurgitate pellets of indigestible fur and bone. Adult birds swallow the microtrash, return to the nest, and regurgitate it for the chicks. Interestingly, no adult condors have had problems with digesting microtrash. It seems that their more fully developed intestinal tracts are able handle the junk that clogs up the younger birds.

Does the microtrash problem simply reflect humanity's greater impact on the environment—in other words, is there just more of civilization's detritus laying around for the birds to get into? Noel Snyder doesn't think so. His data show that condor chicks ingesting microtrash is a new issue. Certainly Carl Koford and other early researchers never saw this behavior. During the 1980s, Snyder rarely found trash at nest sites, and not a single chick ever had a problem with microtrash. But unlike the original wild birds that avoided human structures, released birds today are tamer and more comfortable with human-trafficked areas — places where trash abounds.

It also could be that the birds are just plain bored. The stillborn calves set out as condor food by recovery team members to prevent lead ingestion transform the bird's normal foraging patterns. Instead of roaming the countryside all day looking for their next meal, condors simply fly down from their roost site and eat their fill from a conveniently supplied carcass. Since they only feed once every two or three days, they have plenty of time to kill before eating again. Playing with shiny objects discarded by humans may be an interesting way for smart, curious condors to pass the time.

The recovery team has tried all the obvious remedies. They have cleaned up the trash, especially around the oil rigs near Hopper Mountain. They have scattered bone chips near feeding stations in hopes of diverting the birds toward healthier objects. Unfortunately, nothing has worked. Condors are creatures of habit. Now that the released birds have established this behavior, it is hard to stop it.

If supplemental feeding proves to contribute to the birds's ingestion of microtrash, there is even more urgency to solving the lead ammunition problem and restoring their natural foraging patterns. As Allan Mee watched the chicks in California die from ingesting microtrash, he realized that the recovery team had another challenge on its hands. Meanwhile, no zoo-bred birds had yet to successfully fledge a chick in the wild.

○

March 2003. Biologist Chad Olson slogged along a rock-strewn trail deep in the Grand Canyon, thinking that the name of this inaccessible area—The Inferno—was well deserved. Olson was sweating his way twelve miles into the backcountry to check out a possible condor nest. When the young biologist arrived at the remote canyon from where a pair of condors' radio signals were coming from, he immediately saw a large cave in the face of a lofty cliff. It *had* to be the nest. Soon the male condor swooped in, zoomed along the blood-red cliff—and sailed right past the cave. Moments later, he landed on the lip of another barely visible opening and disappeared inside. He remained there the rest of the day: a good sign that there was an egg inside.

Weeks passed, and Olson monitored the site by following the birds' radio signals rather than repeating the grueling twenty-four-mile round-trip hike. The signals showed the pair taking two- to four-day stints incubating their egg. In May, just when the egg would be expected to hatch, the couple began alternating their shift daily—and sometimes every few hours. They almost certainly had a nestling. If so, it would be the first condor hatched in Arizona in more than one hundred years. The next several months spent raising the young chick would be critical.

In early July, trouble developed: the male's radio signal went silent. Fortunately, he showed up at a feeding station a few days later. Both of his radio transmitters had failed, putting him into "stealth mode" and raising the anxiety level of the watching biologists. If misfortune befell him, he could disappear forever into the Grand Canyon's ancient silence. The recovery team got lucky: a few days later, biologists captured him and fitted his wings with new transmitters.

By mid-August, despite the heat, Olson had to visit the nest. Assuming that the cave held a chick, the juvenile bird would now be walking around the nest and visible from across the canyon. To avoid the sweltering temperatures, Olson and biologist Sophie Osborn hiked into the remote canyon at night. The next morning, they scrambled up a steep talus slope and aimed a spotting scope at the nest cave near the top of a several-hundred-foot cliff. There it was! The young

bird—about the size of an adult condor, but without flight feathers—
strode around a tiny ledge, flapping its wings. It spent the day watching turkey vultures and orange butterflies float by its cliffside home.

By October, the juvenile—now known as Condor 305—was
more than six months old, fully feathered, and almost ready to
fledge. Olson and other biologists now constantly monitored the
cave with spotting scopes. Once or twice a day the chick had periods of tremendous activity, running about and frantically flapping
its wings. It made Olson edgy, however, when it clambered along
the ledge's lip and peered down into the canyon's depths.

Early on the afternoon of November 5, the chick started another round of flapping and hopping. Suddenly it sprang toward a
nearby ledge—and missed. Olson held his breath as it dropped toward the rocks five hundred feet below. The fledgling managed to
partially spread its wings and parachute in a semicontrolled tumble.
Finally it extended its wings for a brief glide before making a surprisingly soft landing on a rock-strewn slope. Olson was beside
himself: the first chick born to captive-bred parents had fledged.

The chick appeared stunned, but soon recovered. Ever curious,
it sauntered over to a nearby yucca plant and began yanking on the
spiky leaves. A couple of hours later, the mother flew into the nest
and saw that her chick had disappeared. She finally spotted it at the
cliff bottom, swooped down, and gave it its first post-fledging meal.

Two days later, Olson tried to trap Condor 305 to attach wing
tags and radio transmitters. He captured it in a handheld net, but the
youngster escaped. The close encounter made the juvenile so wary
that it took more than half a year to finally recapture it. During that
time, Condor 305 was the only bird in the wild without wing tags. A
blood test performed when he was captured showed he was a male.

For months, Condor 305 did not stray far from the nest. He confined himself to short flights around his home canyon and remained
completely dependent on his parents for food. Finally, a group of
other condors paid a visit, and it was not long before Condor 305
followed his new friends to the Kaibab Plateau eleven miles away.

Condor 305 continued to roam the Grand Canyon until March 2005, when his radio transmitters began sending the quick, pulsing mortality signal that indicates a bird has not moved for a considerable time. Olson hated to hear this sound. At first he hoped that it was nothing more serious than a transmitter that had gone astray. But Condor 305's other GPS transmitter also showed no movement. Olson and another biologist set out to investigate. They helicoptered into the maze of canyons and rappelled down a cliff toward the stationary radio pulse. They found Condor 305's body lying on a rocky hillside. A necropsy showed the nearly two-year-old bird was underweight, but there was no obvious cause of death.

○

Condor 305's successful fledging marked another crucial success for the recovery team in their quest to establish a self-sustaining wild condor population. But getting this far had taken years of work and considerable sums of money. Was it worth it?

Saving the condor has certainly been a serious investment. The recovery program's costs have been borne by numerous public and private agencies, so it is hard to come up with an exact figure, but $35 to $40 million is a reasonable estimate. And the recovery effort currently spends roughly $2 million per year—with no end in sight. Could the money be better spent on other, less glamorous endangered species? Or on something else altogether?

"A million here and a million there, and pretty soon you're talking real money," said the late Senator Everett Dirksen. But $40 million over twenty years is not even a blip on the government's budgetary radar. Consider that two decades' worth of spending on the condor recovery program equaled less than six hours of funding for the war in Iraq. Or that shortstop Alex Rodriguez signed a contract for $250 million to entertain baseball fans. Or that Americans spent more than $8 billion last year on liposuctions and facelifts. We have the money. How we spend it is simply a matter of priorities.

Even high-profile conservation programs such as the condor effort get by on modest budgets. Recovery team members often spend uncounted (and sometimes unpaid) hours in primitive conditions, sweating, freezing, and slapping mosquitoes. They don't get rich doing this, and the results are a bargain. In California alone, protecting the condor's habitat helps at least fifty other threatened plants, animals, and reptiles.

Can we afford endangered species preservation efforts like the condor recovery program? Perhaps a better question to ask is why we aren't spending more. The condor exemplifies one of our great modern dilemmas: an extinction epidemic unlike anything our planet has seen in sixty-five million years.

○

Ever since the first microorganisms flickered into existence in a primordial sea, a staggering array of plants and animals have ebbed and flowed across the Earth. And just as death always accompanies life, extinction is evolution's steadfast companion. Of all the living creatures that have emerged on Earth, 99.9 percent have already made their final exit.

Since many species go extinct each year, why should we care if the condor meets its inevitable fate? Why not let the condor, a bird whose low numbers have made it ecologically insignificant for centuries, go in peace? A simple answer is that since we are culpable for the condor's plight, there is a debt to repay. And the condor's status as a "charismatic megafauna" helps call attention to a much larger problem: humanity's destruction of our planet's biodiversity. The rapidly accelerating tempo of extinctions propels us toward a unique moment in history. Stanford University biologist Paul Ehrlich compares the extinction crisis to rivets popping out of an airplane's wing. A few rivets can be lost without harm, but lose enough of them and the wing falls off.

Over the past five hundred million years — the time when complex life forms evolved on Earth — five catastrophic mass extinctions have upended evolution's equilibrium. The best-known among them is called the K-T extinction. During this event, many scientists believe an asteroid slammed into Earth near the Yucatán peninsula's coast, and the resulting cataclysm killed off the dinosaurs. Each of these five extinctions wiped out the dominant life forms and cleared the way for a new burst of evolution. And in each case, it took millions of years for life to recover.

Earth has entered a new and unprecedented era of ecological upheaval known as the sixth extinction. Unlike the previous "Big Five" that were caused by physical events such as asteroid collisions or volcanism, the current mass extinction results from the actions of one species: *Homo sapiens*.

Human-driven extinctions are not new. From Madagascar to New Zealand to North America, the arrival of early humans heralded the end of most of the large animals. The pace has rapidly accelerated. A combination of overpopulation, consumption, and technology are fueling the sixth extinction.

There are approximately 1.5 million identified species worldwide, but millions more remain unknown to science. Each year about ten thousand new species are "discovered." Groups such as birds and mammals are well catalogued; most new species are life forms such as arachnids or microbes. Estimates of the total number of the Earth's species vary considerably. Ten million? Fifteen million? No one knows. But while uncertainty about the precise numbers remains, the aberrant and alarmingly high extinction rate is well documented.

Columbia University biologist Stuart Pimm's pioneering work compared the normal "background" extinction rate found in the fossil record and other research with the current wave of species loss. The present extinction level ranges somewhere between one thousand and ten thousand times the usual background rate—and it is rising rapidly. With the continuing destruction of the species-rich rain forests, Pimm estimates that extinctions will increase by as much as tenfold in the next half century. If that happens, half the world's species will be gone.

Not surprisingly, habitat destruction leads the way in causing species loss. It is one reason that Carl Koford placed so much value on preserving the condor's habitat. Since species are not distributed evenly over the Earth, certain areas—such as tropical forests—are biodiversity hotspots. Half the world's tropical rain forests have already been burned or logged, and the clearing continues unabated. In 2004 alone an area in the Amazon nearly the size of Belgium was cut down. Most extinctions in such places are never even observed or recorded.

Invasive species—non-native biological invaders introduced into habitats—are another potent force undermining the integrity of our ecosystems and driving the sixth extinction. Biological invasions were once a rare event: a species would occasionally drift on an ocean current or be carried by a bird to a new land. Invasive species now tag along in the ballast water of ships or the cargo holds of aircraft. This human-induced rapid movement of species is unprecedented. These alien intruders, accidentally or intentionally spread by humans, ravage habitats that have not evolved natural defenses against them. Once established, invasive species are often impossible to eradicate. The spread of these invaders leaves the natural environment more homogenized and therefore less stable.

Another factor driving the sixth extinction is the overexploitation of natural resources. A long list of species has disappeared because of human greed. These days, one need look no further than the depleted fishing grounds in the world's oceans for an example of short-term exploitation leading to longer-term consequences.

In the coming decades, many bird species may face a dilemma much like the condor's. A 2004 forecast by researchers at the Stanford University Center for Conservation Biology reported that unless things change, about ten percent of the ten thousand bird species on Earth will go extinct by the end of the century. An additional fifteen percent will be so reduced that they will no longer be ecologically significant. The secondary effects of the potential loss of so many bird species on seed dispersal, plant pollination, and insect consumption are unknown.

The sixth extinction has already altered human existence. Our hope lies in developing an understanding that humans are not separate from nature, we *are* nature. We must make room for other species, whether it is a tiny snail or a giant condor. By ensuring their continuing existence, we sustain the future of all life.

Ironically, the greater our powers become, the more we are rendered impotent. Humankind inherited the greatest diversity of species in Earth's history. Our challenge is to restrain our population and our technology in order to preserve the one place in the universe where *Homo sapiens* can thrive.

Writer Jan DeBlieu said, "To be a conservationist is to be an eternal optimist. Pessimism serves no purpose, not when you are trying to change the world." And yet, the daunting problems we confront can create paralysis. What can one person do?

"When we try to pick out anything by itself, we find it hitched to everything else in the universe," John Muir said. The condor is one good place to start. Ian McMillan, the feisty rancher-naturalist who opposed hands-on condor management, got it right when he said, "The real importance of saving such things as condors is not so much that we need condors, as that we need to save condors."

Thousands of people who see their first condor think; *This bird must be saved.* Success with the condor, once a long-shot gamble, now largely rests on political negotiations, not technical challenges. If we pull the condor from the fires of extinction, it augurs well for preserving and restoring more of our natural world. We can stem the tide of environmental destruction one habitat, one species, one wing beat at a time. And this gives us the courage to dream large. Is there any other choice?

○

An early stop in my condor research was one of the world's finest repositories of natural artifacts: the American Museum of Natural

History in New York City. I went there to learn about condors, and ended up finding an unexpected aperture that cast light on the extinction crisis.

Visitors enter the museum via a colossal rotunda housing a dinosaur display. In it, a brontosaurus rears up on its hind legs defending against an attacking allosaurous. A baby brontosaurus—it is bigger than an elephant—crouches behind the parent's tail. These behemoths dwarf a condor, but they are actually distant relatives. Condors and other birds trace their ancestry to dinosaurs. When we look skyward, we see the living descendents of those "terrible lizards" flying overhead.

I spend the morning with Peter Capainolo in the Ornithology Department. Although we are on the opposite side of the continent from condor country, the museum has an excellent collection of condor eggs, study skins, and research material. Capainolo takes me to see a mounted condor locked in a cabinet in the collections area. We kneel to examine the bird, which fills the cabinet's bottom half. This condor is old, probably from the early 1900s, and looks faded and lifeless. The head and neck are poorly crafted from a plaster cast, and its feet and legs are a shocking shade of purple. After discussing the specimen, I notice a black-and-white bird next to it. It's more than 30 inches tall and has a large bill.

"A great auk?"

Capainolo nods. "Went extinct in 1844."

It's as if I'm in a time machine and a visitor from the past has unexpectedly materialized. My fingertips graze the bird's white breast. Immense numbers of this penguinlike bird once inhabited the Atlantic Ocean, especially near Greenland, Iceland, and eastern Canada. Like the condor, it laid just one egg at a time. These agile swimmers were flightless, which made them easy pickings for sailors, who slaughtered them into extinction. Only eighty preserved skins still exist, and this is one of the world's few mounted specimens.

I slowly stand up, taking in the smaller birds on the top shelves, and suddenly the nature of this cabinet's holdings dawns on me. A label taped to the door reads "Rare and Extinct." We're looking at a species graveyard.

I remember as a child my father reading aloud a chapter from Rachel Carson's *Silent Spring*. When I went to bed that evening, I listened to the summer night reverberate with crickets and tried to imagine a muted darkness. It seemed impossible to conjure up such a stillness. I remember how I struggled in vain to comprehend the infinite universe, where one could spin through the black firmament forever. When I envisioned a silent spring, my mind reeled with vertigo.

"What's this one?"

"Passenger pigeon." Capainolo hands me the mounted specimen, and I'm struck by the subtle blue-gray watercolor-wash of its feathers. The passenger pigeon was once *the most common bird in North America*. A mere two hundred years ago, the roar of wings from their seemingly inexhaustible flocks drowned out the reports of hunters' guns.

"Have a look over here." Capainolo opens a nearby drawer and removes a passenger pigeon study skin stuffed with cotton. "The male had a cinnamon-colored breast." The study skin floats on my hand. A necklace of iridescent feathers rings the bird's neck. I'm not sure what I feel: sadness, awe, or a wave of queasiness that this is all that remains.

We return to the cabinet of ghosts. Here's an ivory-billed woodpecker, a bird so spectacular that some called it the "Lord God bird," which is what people would exclaim upon seeing it. This specimen looks shrunken and anemic compared to the pictures I've seen. Logging destroyed most of the bird's habitat, and for decades it was presumed extinct. Miraculously, ornithologists from Cornell may have recently rediscovered the ivory-billed woodpecker in a swampy, snake-infested nature reserve in Arkansas. Against all odds, this king of the woodpeckers might yet be resurrected from the dead.

A middle shelf holds an Eskimo curlew, a long-legged shorebird with a scimitar-shaped bill. It gained the nickname "doughbird" because of the thick layers of fat it accumulated for migration. The Eskimo curlew was once one of the most numerous birds in Canada and, like the passenger pigeon, its panoramic flocks obscured the sun. These easy-to-shoot birds were considered a delicacy, and uncontrolled hunting annihilated them.

I pick up a Carolina parakeet, once the jewel of American skies. The rainbow burst of tropical yellows and oranges on the bird's head have dulled with age, but the body feathers still retain elegant shades of blue tinged with startling green. Farmers considered these birds pests because they ate fruit and grain. The species eventually succumbed to shooting and deforestation. I hold this treasure and try to fix each detail in my memory. It's the only chance I'll get.

In thinking about what this cabinet represents, an unexpected word comes to mind: *obscene*. There are still more birds—a heath hen, another common bird of the American Northeast that was hunted to oblivion; a Bachman's warbler, the victim of habitat loss . . . I've seen enough. I thank Capainolo, and he locks the cabinet. We leave this room where nothing moves, our shoes scuffing across a linoleum floor and fluorescent lights buzzing overhead. Everything smells of mothballs.

On my way out of the museum, I notice a quote from Theodore Roosevelt on the rotunda wall:

> *The nation behaves well if it treats*
> *the natural resources as assets*
> *which it must turn over to the next generation*
> *increased and not impaired in value.*

What will future generations say about a culture founded on the bones of uncounted bison and the dusty feathers of extinct birds? In the end, we will be remembered not by what we built, but by what we conserved.

I walk outside into the New York City bustle, still thinking about that condor with purple legs. I'm glad the recovery effort's successes give us a good chance of bequeathing to future generations real condors. We should leave behind more than just shadows in the sky.

○

A sustainable wild condor population is built one bird at a time. But not all condors are created equal. No matter how objective scientists try to be, the original wild birds captured in the 1980s hold a singular appeal. Despite all the data collection and all the "thinking with one's head," there can be a subtle undertow of the heart.

Of all the last wild condors, there is a single bird—the one most watched and studied—that evokes the most sentiment: AC9. By 2002 AC9 had spent fifteen years in the Los Angeles Zoo and had sired fourteen offspring. His genes were well represented in the captive flock. Talks began about releasing him to the wild. Not everyone agreed. In the opinion of longtime condor biologist Dave Clendenen, the wild birds should not be released until the program no longer depends on feeding stations to minimize lead poisoning. He believes that the wild birds need to share their invaluable knowledge with zoo-bred condors to teach them how to forage and to act. Noel Snyder makes the same case, convinced that the one hope the program has of ever getting really appropriate wild behavior is from the knowledge of the remaining historical birds. "Don't waste them," he warns. "Don't put them out in the wild under less than optimal conditions."

But there is a driving passion to release at least some of the wild birds. Not only can they act as mentors for captive-bred birds, but there is the nudge of conscience that it is the right thing to do. Over the years, Jan Hamber sometimes visited the handful of original wild birds held in the zoos. Although a lifelong scientist and dispassionate by training, she, too, felt the inexorable force pulling them toward freedom. She would stand by their condorminiums and remember what Carl Koford had said: A condor in a zoo is a pitiful sight. She thought of the night she called in the team to capture AC9 and remembered hearing the cannon net explode the next morning. Sometimes she would send a mental message to the caged condors: *Someday, you're going to go back out.*

13

Homeward Bound

MY FRIEND JOE COOK and I are on our way to the first Central California condor release at Pinnacles National Monument in 2003. It should be a momentous event, but we're not sure the gods are with us. A sky filled with sullen clouds obscures the December dawn and threatens the day's plans. If a storm front moves in, the birds won't be flying.

We drive inland past Mission San Juan Bautista, where two hundred years ago padres baptized Native Americans forced from their ancestral lands. Until the past century, condors still flew free in these skies. Nowadays, fast-food restaurants have replaced the mission village, and there are no condors. But if all goes well, after today's release, the condors will be back.

We turn south into the backcountry. Despite the uncertain weather, a line of cars fills the two-lane road leading into Pinnacles. We are not the only ones who want to watch six young condors fly free.

We park and hike a mile through a valley of manzanita and gray pines to a natural amphitheater, where rangers have set up an observation area. This grassy glen offers a clear view of the flight pen, which is perched atop a ridge less than a mile away. Hundreds of people stream toward the viewing area as if they are on a pilgrimage, talking of the condor's return to this wilderness after a long century's absence.

For now the rain keeps its distance. I train my spotting scope on the flight-pen ridge that is bathed in pastel winter light. Two young condors are already up and clinging to the mesh enclosure, spreading their wings to the chilly gusts. I invite a father and his daughter to have a look. The man lifts the young girl to the scope's eyepiece, and the brilliant view of the giant birds soaring on the netting makes her gasp. "Big birds, Daddy!"

The release, managed by the Ventana Wildlife Society, is planned for mid-morning. As a prelude, a collection of windblown dignitaries speak into a portable sound system to address the crowd. U.S. Congressman Sam Farr says that spending money to save the condor is an example of government functioning at its best. Kelly Sorenson from the Ventana Wildlife Society describes the flight pen's double-door arrangement. As soon as a calf carcass attracts one of the birds into the passageway, the inside door will be shut and the outside door opened. One bird will be released at a time—the poor mentor bird will stay behind.

Now we wait. The wind grows stronger, the clouds darken, but no birds fly. By late morning, with the weather worsening, Sorenson announces that the release is postponed. It seems to be a metaphor for the condor recovery program: nothing happens quickly. Joe and I hang around to chat with some birders we know. Joe's brought along an old T-shirt commemorating the 1981 Condor Watch and Tequila Bust, an annual Southern California gathering back in the seventies and eighties at which condor aficionados would come together to count the birds, argue about how to save them, and drink a little tequila. It's too cold to wear a T-shirt today, so Joe has draped it over one of our folding chairs. A woman with short gray hair spots the T-shirt and stops to reminisce with him. Not knowing her, I continue talking with the other birders.

But when she overhears that I wrote this morning's front-page newspaper article on the release, we begin discussing condors. It is immediately apparent that she knows a lot about the birds. I am also impressed that she has driven more than two hundred miles from

Santa Barbara for the release. She explains that she is a condor biologist, and that these days she works part-time at the Santa Barbara
Museum of Natural History. I extend my hand and introduce myself.

She smiles. "I'm Jan Hamber."

I recognize her name from some of my condor research. We continue chatting, and I ask if she has attended other condor releases.

"Oh, I've gone to so many."

"What was your most memorable release?"

"Last year. When AC9 was set free."

○

May 1, 2002, dawned clear and balmy, and Jan could not have
been happier. She'd been hoping for this day ever since that doubt-
filled evening in 1987 when she drove to a little Union 76 gas station and placed the fateful call to condor trapper Pete Bloom. So
much time had gone by. How could it be, Jan wondered, that she
was now a grandmother in her seventies? It seemed a lifetime ago
that she had peered through a spotting scope to watch the newborn
AC9 in his nest cave, begging his parents for food. Despite all the
setbacks and heartbreaks and political battles, the audacious effort
to save the condor was succeeding. And Jan's fifteen-year-old vow
that AC9 would once again fly free was just hours from fulfillment.

A crowd of more than one hundred people gathered at Koford's
Observation Post on Hopper Mountain, directly across the canyon
from the crumbling sandstone of Arundell Cliffs. A few days earlier
AC9 had been helicoptered to a flight pen perched on the clifftop.
Accompanying him were three juvenile zoo-bred birds.

Jan hiked out to the observation post with her ten-year-old
grandson, Zachary. She ambled along, watching with pleasure as
Zachary identified plants and drew them in his sketchbook. Jan
didn't mind dawdling. People came to condor releases expecting
the birds to step from the flight pen and immediately spring into the
air. Jan knew that the condors were in no hurry—the birds usually
stood around for hours.

Lining the ridge was a cluster of reporters and photographers, along with scores of people who had worked with the condor program. Jan smiled at seeing all her old friends. Like her, many of them had known AC9 all of his life.

At mid-morning, the enclosure's door opened, and AC9 emerged into the netted area on the clifftop. The three juvenile birds followed. Unlike past releases, where the net had been completely removed, this time only one corner of the mesh had been lifted to allow the birds to go free. The three young condors soon discovered the opening and wandered out to explore the clifftop. But after fifteen years of captivity, when given his chance for freedom, AC9 seemed to be saying, "I think I'll pass." Two hours went by, and AC9 still did not leave the netted enclosure. Jan could not help smiling at the irony. As she waited, a stream of reporters came to interview her. Jan made a point to talk about how AC9's release symbolized the importance of promoting and supporting endangered species work. AC9's return to the wild marked a victory for more than just a single bird or even a single species.

Noon approached, and still AC9 did not move. Not wanting to disappoint the crowd, an intern stepped into the pen and shooed AC9 out the opening. It was not graceful, but who cared? There he was, unfettered at last.

Jan thought about what a difference there was between this sunny moment surrounded by family and friends and that frosty evening long ago when it had been just her, the last wild condor, and the inexorable ticking of the extinction clock.

AC9 spread his wings and eased into the air. A buzz ran through the crowd. Fingers pointed, binoculars raised. Jan remembered her promise: *One day AC9 will again fly free.* And there he was, winging along the ridge, the crowd applauding and cheering. Jan watched AC9 circle higher over the cliffs and canyons of his youth —*free, free, free at last.*

◯

Since his release, AC9 has continued to ride the wind over his old territory. His freedom represents another heartening development in a long string of condor program victories. More than twenty-five years ago, Kenneth Brower wrote with a touch of hyperbole: "When man and condor meet today, it is with a glance of mutual appraisal, each to see whether the other is yet extinct."

Since that tenuous time, the recovery program has increased the number of condors by more than a magnitude, from a desperate low of twenty-two birds to a rapidly growing total of nearly three hundred. More than one hundred twenty-five condors now fly free over the western United States and Baja California. Each year, captive-breeding facilities at the Los Angeles Zoo, the San Diego Wild Animal Park, the Oregon Zoo, and the Peregrine Fund's World Center for Birds of Prey in Idaho each reliably produce a new group of condors. Released condors now breeding in the wild also add an occasional chick to this number.

Viewed from where the recovery program stood in 1982, with no captive-breeding population and only a sketchy understanding of condor biology, the future looks bright. The recovery program has achieved some remarkable milestones: the first hatching of a zoo-bred bird, the triumphant return of California condors to America's skies, the successful fledging of a bird born in the wild, and the release of AC8 and AC9.

Back in the 1980s, many biologists would have been delighted to face the problems the recovery effort now confronts. The condor program's eventual goal of two separate self-sustaining wild populations—one in California and one in Arizona—of at least 150 birds each is no longer a long shot. What bodes especially well for the recovery effort today is that the chief obstacle blocking success—removing toxic lead bullets from the environment—is a political issue that can be resolved, not an intractable biological problem.

The reason condors now grace our skies can be summed up in two words: captive breeding. This technique has also been tried—with mixed results—with other endangered species, such as the red wolf, the black-footed ferret, the Puerto Rican parrot, and the whooping crane. Despite the success with the California condor, most biologists regard captive breeding as a last resort. Still, the method holds a certain allure: the bird-in-the-hand syndrome. In a zoo, veterinarians can shelter an endangered species from the dangers of the wild, keeping them well-fed and disease-free. At the same time, they can preserve whatever genetic diversity the species still has rather than risk inbreeding in a tiny wild population. But wildlife scientists agree that captive-breeding programs are at best only a palliative and that an insidious danger awaits animals held for too long behind moats and bars.

Evolution does not cease just because an animal is in captivity. Endangered species confined in zoos undergo physical and psychological changes that, within a few generations, may render them mere zoo curiosities, incapable of returning to the wild. Zookeepers have discovered that with short-lived insects, such as endangered butterflies, evolutionary changes occur so rapidly that captive breeding is almost useless. Condor biologist Jesse Grantham contends that this is a key reason to expeditiously wean the condor away from intensive management practices that foster unwanted behavior changes. "We don't want to save the bird but lose the species," he said.

Zoos sometimes compare themselves to modern-day arks, sheltering endangered species from the storm of the sixth extinction. This may make for catchy press releases, but captive breeding provides no antidote for the destruction of habitat, the spread of invasive species, or the overexploitation of resources. At best, a captive-breeding program buys time, as it did for the condor. But as difficult as it can be to take animals into captivity, the real challenge lies in successfully returning a species to the wild.

The first captive-bred condors were released into a bizarre environment: it was as if a catastrophe had wiped out their species. With no knowledgeable adult birds to teach them how to live, those pioneer condors had to learn how to survive and how to establish a new social structure all over again. It has not been easy, and the recovery program still struggles to return them to truly wild behavior. The condor program's greatest successes—among them the remarkable reproductive rate of zoo birds—have come when the bird was completely under human control. Once returned to the wild, condors are at the mercy of a damaged environment and the vicissitudes of nature.

The condor effort exemplifies the problems inherent in rereleasing endangered species back into a toxic environment. What initially threatened the species must first be eliminated; otherwise, the original problem will be re-created. In the condor's case, not pushing ahead to solve the lead issue means sustaining an expensive stop-gap program.

Just as a captive animal population undergoes detrimental evolutionary changes, long-term recovery programs can also suffer from a drift in their goals. As years pass, and interagency politics grow more byzantine, a recovery effort's objectives may shift away from saving the species and toward preserving jobs and perpetuating itself. Sometimes program leaders lose sight of the fact that vested interests have undermined their real mission.

Perhaps the greatest lesson from the condor recovery program is to not allow an endangered species population to get so desperately low. A crisis mentality, where the worst problems are only addressed at the eleventh hour, results in the most expensive and least effective approach to species preservation. Instead of rescuing one species at a time, it makes better sense to preserve entire habitats. Once a habitat is gone—or even seriously altered—it is impossible to re-create. Often, what has been lost is not even known.

○

I had one last place to go: the wild mountains near my old hometown of Santa Paula. In the fall of 2005 I planned a visit to the Hopper Mountain National Wildlife Refuge adjacent to the Sespe Condor Sanctuary, Southern California's primary release site. I wanted to talk with biologists about the area's releases, to see where

Carl Koford had studied condors, and to visit the place where the first captive-bred birds returned to freedom.

Those were the logical reasons, but I had other, less tangible motives. I wanted the satisfaction of once again seeing condors flying near that wind-whipped ridge behind Santa Paula Peak where I spotted my first birds. And I wanted to view the one bird I had spent so much time researching, the bird I knew best. I wanted to see the quintessential condor: AC9. Rationally speaking, seeing AC9 was of little consequence. He would not look different from any of the dozens of other condors I had already seen. And yet, when I headed for Hopper Mountain, all I could think about was that bird.

○

It is raining—again. Two weeks earlier, wet weather had canceled my Hopper Mountain trip. Hopper Mountain's dirt roads turn to a muddy, impassible mess after a storm. This misty October morning does not look much better.

I meet Denise Stockton, the refuge's information and education specialist, at the Hopper Mountain Complex office in Ventura. Stockton has planned to spend the day showing me around the refuge, which is closed to the public.

I cast a doubtful glance skyward.

"Let's give it a try," Stockton says. She pulls on her brown U.S. Fish & Wildlife Service fleece jacket, and we climb into her SUV. Soon we're driving east on Highway 126, a route I've taken hundreds of times, and in fifteen minutes Santa Paula's familiar exits are flashing past. The citrus groves carpeting the Santa Clara River Valley drip with fog, and clouds obscure Santa Paula Peak. Another fifteen minutes and we're in Fillmore, where Stockton exits and turns north into the mountains. She drops the SUV into four-wheel drive, and we climb a twisting dirt road four thousand feet into a tapestry of clouds.

Stockton navigates the hairpin turns slowly. On our left, the road plunges to the silver ribbon of Sespe Creek hundreds of yards below. "We had an intern drive off this road. Right . . . there." Stockton points. "Her Blazer flipped seven times tumbling into the gorge. We found her just before dark and airlifted her out. She was lucky to survive. Got to pay attention here."

Stockton calls ahead on her two-way radio to let the field crew know we are on our way. Every few minutes, radio chatter among condor observers punctuates our conversation.

Female voice: "I've got 155 over the Pinnacles right now heading your way."

Male voice replies: "Roger. I'm already picking up the signal."

I ask, "Any chance we might see AC9 today?"

"He's up here," Stockton says. "We'll see if any of the observers have him on their radio frequencies." She leans forward and peers up through the windshield. "But with this weather . . ."

The mist has turned to a steady drizzle. Despite the early rains, the grass-covered mountains retain a stubborn summer brown that is broken only by scattered green islands of oak and coffeeberry. As we ascend, Stockton explains how biologists and interns track released condors at the refuge, constantly monitoring the birds' behavior and well-being. Stockton's husband is the supervising biologist at Hopper Mountain.

We are bouncing up the same road where young Carl Koford carried in boxes of groceries and supplies. It is the road that Jan Hamber and others drove to see the first release of captive-bred condors in 1992, as well as the releases of both AC8 and AC9.

An oil truck approaches, and Stockton eases into a turnout to let the giant rig lumber past. Although this is called a wildlife refuge, the petroleum industry is ever-present. Pipelines snake down steep slopes, and dozens of derricks set on oil pads are bulldozed into the hillsides.

At last we reach the mountaintop. The visibility drops to less than one hundred yards—not exactly condor-watching weather. Dark oaks flank the road. Stockton stops to point out the wreck of an oil worker's cabin where Carl Koford once lived. The tin roof and wooden beams have collapsed into a heap of twisted metal and

smashed lumber. Directly across the road, an oil pad has been lev-
eled into the hillside. It looks preposterous, a shameless collection
of pipes, tanks, and derricks. This is wilderness? I can only imagine what Koford would say.

"We're almost to our first stop," Stockton says, making another
radio call. Out of the fog emerges a large gravel pullout that serves
as an observation post, and in it, a parked truck. Condor intern Lisa
Drake steps from the truck and greets us with a damp smile. She
has tucked her hair under a wool cap and the mist fogs her glasses.
She carries a yard-long, three-pronged antenna. Drake grips the
handle, which is wrapped with electrician's tape, and points the antenna toward the fog. "We've got a bunch of birds nearby," she
says. "The trick will be to see them."

She punches numbers into a keypad on a receiver that looks like
a field telephone from World War II, and we hear a steady clicking.
Drake nods. "Good strong signal. My guess is that they're roosting
on Koford's Snag." She gestures toward an opaque white curtain.

While we shuffle from one foot to another in the blowing fog,
Drake describes how she is part of a team of four interns under the
direction of a field biologist that monitors the birds. It is not a job
for everyone: interns spend ten-day shifts up here, combining biology with more mundane chores such as repairing roads and haul-
ing calf carcasses.

"Today we're set up to trap Condor 155," she says. "He's been
acting strangely, and we want to check him out to see what's wrong.
But with this weather, I'm not sure if the birds will be flying much."
As Drake scribbles notes into her logbook, the stiffening breeze
lifts the fog, revealing an oil pad on the hillside right in front of us.
Nearly a dozen green-and-yellow derricks spring into view. A sub-
tle odor drifts on the wind, triggering a childhood memory of the
Long Beach petroleum fields. Our view continues expanding, and
I hurry to the SUV for my binoculars.

"Right there," Stockton says. "Koford's Snag." A giant dead
tree materializes out of the gloom. It is several hundred yards away,

and through binoculars I discern several large black shapes sitting on the branches. I count eight condors.

"Any of them AC9?" I ask.

Drake punches in the bird's radio frequency, and we hear an insistent clicking. "Yup, he's one of them."

But we are too far away to see the birds' wing tags, much less read their numbers. It's very quiet, just three humans watching eight condors on a foggy mountaintop. The clouds lower again, and the scene fades to white.

I've seen AC9—sort of.

We wait a few more minutes, but the fog persists, so Stockton and I leave Drake at the observation post and drive off to visit a flight pen. At noon we take a break at an old ranch house that serves as the recovery team's base of operations for Hopper Mountain. The main house is a rambling affair surrounded by a number of outbuildings. A large living room holds several battered sofas and cluttered desks. As we walk from room to room, the floor gains and loses elevation. These spartan quarters are home for biologists and interns during their time in the field. A bear hunter named Ari Hopper first moved here after the Civil War, and a ranching family owned this house during the 1930s and 1940s, when Carl Koford was a frequent guest.

After lunch, we wander the ranch-house grounds. An acorn woodpecker, its black-and-white head sporting a bright red cap, belts out a laughing call: *wheka, wheka wheka*. A few hopeful patches of blue sky appear, and two juvenile condors cruise overhead.

Stockton drives me to another observation post overlooking a grassy valley. To our right towers an ashen sandstone ridge called the Pinnacles: striated bands of sedimentary rock pitching and twisting through the earthen hues of autumn grass. A shaft of sunlight pours over this crumpled monolith, and five juvenile condors swoop over the peaks and begin circling the valley in front of us. The break in the weather has brought out the birds.

"That's our trap site," Stockton says, gesturing toward a cage-like structure of chain-link fencing set in the middle of the flat, grassy vale. "One of the sides is made out of netting that's held up by a rope. The rope leads to the blind over there . . ." She points to a four-by-eight plywood shack about a hundred yards from the cage. "A biologist is in there, waiting. There's a calf carcass inside the trap, and if Condor 155 enters the cage, the biologist will pull the rope, releasing the net and capturing our bird."

More condors emerge out of the clouds, and soon there are so many birds spiraling and spinning over the baited walk-in trap that it takes a few minutes to get an accurate count: sixteen condors. We're looking at what was not very long ago nearly three-quarters of the world's entire California condor population. A pair of ravens struts around the calf carcass, but the condors do not come down to feed.

Drake radios to Stockton that one of the circling birds is AC9. But the condors are a third of a mile away, so there is no chance of identifying him. Another near miss.

We move on, and an hour later, we spot five condors circling a canyon just off the road. Stockton radios up to Drake, and she confirms that one of them is AC9. In an instant, I am out of the SUV with binoculars in hand, scanning the birds. Two of them have dark heads—immatures—so I concentrate on the other three. I can see the number tags, I can *almost* read the numbers. The birds drop lower, tantalizingly close. One condor lowers its legs, using them as rudders to steer through the bumpy air. We can hear the wind humming in its enormous flight feathers. Then the birds drift higher, their black wings fading to gray, and disappear into the alabaster sky. We wait, but the condors are gone. Soon it begins to drizzle. We're cold and wet; it's time to head back to Ventura.

Stockton reminds me to put on my seatbelt, and we lurch back down the mountain. "Are you disappointed you didn't identify AC9?" she asks. I shake my head, feeling curiously at peace. Maybe it is better this way, to leave AC9 a bit enigmatic. I remember that moment thirty years ago when my first two condors flashed by on

Santa Paula Peak; I remember fearing that I would never have such a moment again.

Because of the quixotic quest to save this species, just today we have seen as many condors as once existed in the entire world. Thanks to good science—and good luck—the mythical birds are back home. The sky that Jan Hamber described as empty following AC9's capture once again embraces our largest bird.

One last time I glance back up at the distant, cloud-shrouded mountains. There is not a bird to be seen. But I know that AC9 and the other condors are there, circling . . . circling: black gossamer sky giants, the wind song of their flight feathers alive with a wild melody.

AFTERWORD

THREE CONDORS SWOOP low over the volcanic peaks of Pinnacles National Park, weaving their way across a winter sky. It's January 2023, and my son and I are hiking the familiar Condor Gulch Trail, the air fragrant with chaparral and rain-dampened earth. It's so quiet I can feel my pulse, which quickens a bit at the sight of these regal fliers.

As I watch the condors, I feel a tug of nostalgia. It was here on a blustery day two decades ago that I came to report on the first Pinnacles condor release, one of the early stories I wrote about the bird. Reintroducing condors at Pinnacles was a milestone in the recovery program, and since then many more condors have been released here.

We take our time as we hike skyward toward the rugged spires, delighting in the presence of the three birds. Crafting those early condor stories ignited my passion for these extraordinary beings and the humans trying to save them and led to the writing of this book. Since then, I've continued covering the condor's recovery, and I'm happy to report that these days nearly 350 condors fly free over western North America. When you add in the additional condors in captivity, the total population now approaches 560 birds. That's nearly double the number of condors that existed in the world when this book was first published in 2006.

Yet despite the increasing population and other positive advances, the condor remains critically endangered, and challenges on several fronts continue. Join me as we look at recent developments in the remarkable saga of the return of the condor.

○

As the sun dawns on the otherworldly landscape of Zion National Park, it illuminates towering sandstone cliffs that greet the day with a symphony of colors. In May 2019 in a small cave on one of these radiant cliff faces, a pair of condors hatched a chick. Although wild-born chicks are now an annual occurrence, this one was special. That little ball of fluff the parent birds were cuddling and feeding was the 1,000th bird hatched since the beginning of the California Condor Recovery Program four decades earlier, a time when the future of the condor hung in the balance.

It's striking to contemplate that in 1987, when biologist Jan Hamber helped capture AC9, the last free-flying wild bird, California condors had never been bred in captivity. When the recovery program began, the prospects of any births—much less 1,000 of them—were far from certain. Jan told me recently, "At the time, so much was unknown about the species. And it was an open question whether the condor could be saved."

The birth of Condor 1K, as he was named, was yet another landmark in the decades-long effort toward reestablishing self-sustaining wild condor populations. Rather than becoming a museum relic, these marvelous birds are still riding the thermals over western skies.

○

Of the original twenty-seven wild California condors at the heart of the do-or-die captive-breeding effort, the best-known and most studied was AC9. His story wove its way through this book's narrative, from the first page to the last. After the cannon net exploded over him on Easter morning in 1987, he spent fifteen years in captivity until his release back to the canyons and crags of his youth. He soon found a mate, and they nested together eight times in Southern California until she died in 2015. In the next breeding season AC9 paired with a new female, and in 2016 they were raising their first chick together.

Then AC9 went missing.

The first hint of trouble came when biologists tracking AC9 via his GPS transmitter noticed that, at a time when he should have been making long foraging flights to find food for his chick, his movements suddenly became limited to a remote canyon in the Sespe Wilderness.

On June 30, all transmissions ceased.

Worried biologists searched the area of AC9's last GPS signals, but it proved fruitless. On July 8 they entered his nest site located in a small cave. His mate and chick were in good health, but the biologists found no sign of AC9. Images from a game camera installed in the nesting cavity showed that two weeks had passed since AC9's last visit, confirming their worst fears.

If they don't find a body, the U.S. Fish & Wildlife Service lets a year pass with no sightings or transmissions before officially declaring a bird lost. The silent months drifted past and on July 11, 2017, the sad announcement was made, prompting an outpouring of grief. It was the end of an era.

We will never know for sure how AC9 died. At age thirty-six, he still had the potential for many more years of life. Perhaps he suffered an injury, or maybe—like so many condors—he succumbed to lead poisoning. Whatever the cause, AC9 holds a unique place in condor history, the bird who flew solo in an empty sky— the last wild condor, winging his way toward an uncertain future.

○

These days, you don't have to talk with a condor biologist very long before you're likely to hear the words *lead poisoning*. The single biggest limiting factor to the condor's recovery comes from the birds inadvertently ingesting spent lead bullet fragments. That was true when I wrote this book and, sadly, it is still true today. What *has* changed is additional research that gives us an even better understanding of the deleterious effects of spent lead ammunition on condors, other wildlife, and humans.

From 1992—when the first captive-bred condors were released—through the end of 2020, lead poisoning has killed 50 percent of all birds with a known cause of death. Moreover, it's only the constant testing and treating of condors for lead poisoning that keeps the toll from rising even higher. With the ongoing losses from lead, releasing captive-bred birds from zoos is helping replenish the wild population.

A comprehensive study in 2012 found that poisoning in condors from lead ammunition is of "epidemic proportion." The continual exposure to harmful levels of lead requires costly and continuous intensive management efforts. The study's primary author, Myra Finkelstein, a research toxicologist at the University of California, Santa Cruz, said, "We will never have a self-sustaining wild condor population if we don't solve this problem."

The condor's slow reproduction rate—usually only one chick every other year—makes it challenging for the species to rebound from the unnatural number of deaths caused by lead poisoning. But many other birds and animals suffer as well. A 2022 nationwide study of lead poisoning in bald eagles and golden eagles found nearly 50 percent of the birds sampled showed evidence of repeated exposure to lead, which is impacting the populations of these iconic birds. The eagles sometimes scavenge on carrion, and lead poisoning typically occurs when a bird inadvertently eats lead bullet fragments. Lead poisoning affects more than 100 *other* species, and each year takes an indiscriminate and needless toll on wildlife.

Furthermore, there has been a growing recognition of the danger humans face when eating wild game shot with lead bullets. I reported on the story of North Dakota physician and hunter William Cornatzer, whose concern over how lead bullets shattered and spread widely in game animals and their deadly consequences for condors led to critical new discoveries. He wondered: *Are people who eat hunter-shot game also at risk?* Cornatzer radiographed packages of venison donated to food banks and found many of them laced with deadly lead fragments that were so small a person would not know they were eating them. His discovery led to the Centers for Disease Control and Prevention conducting a study showing a link between people who ate hunter-shot wild game and higher blood-lead levels. Other research from around the world has shown similar results. The World Health Organization has made clear the danger, stating that *no known level of lead exposure is considered safe*—and young children and pregnant women are particularly vulnerable.

In 2013, thirty leading scientific experts issued a consensus statement describing lead ammunition as the "greatest, largely unregulated source of lead knowingly discharged into the environment." The statement describes the risks of lead-based ammunition to wildlife and humans and calls for its reduction and eventual elimination.

Fortunately, solid copper bullets offer an excellent alternative. Because copper bullets don't shatter into hundreds of toxic fragments like lead bullets, they don't kill twice. With a solution at hand, conservation, hunting, and public health constituencies have mounted efforts to transition to nonlead ammunition. This had been done before with the successful 1991 nationwide ban of lead shot for waterfowl hunting that was poisoning millions of birds.

The push for nonlead bullets has taken two approaches. The first is voluntary cooperation. For years, condor recovery program partners and others have operated education and outreach efforts and even given away free copper bullets to encourage hunters and ranchers to make the switch. The second strategy is through legislation and regulation. California has taken the lead, first banning hunting with lead bullets in regions where condors had been released, and a few years later extending the ban statewide, which took full effect in 2019.

Thus far, neither approach has been a panacea. Asking for voluntary compliance depends on most hunters and ranchers understanding the problem and making the switch, something that remains a work in progress. On the other hand, laws banning lead are hard to enforce over vast public wild areas and on private lands where condors roam but wildlife officers don't. Unfortunately, both approaches have been hampered by a lack of availability of copper ammunition. Meanwhile, lead bullets remain legal for target practice and are easily obtainable.

The California legislation is still relatively new, and its rollout was complicated when the pandemic, which arrived just months after the law took effect, spiked the demand for guns and ammunition, leaving store shelves empty of any kind of bullets and compounding the copper bullet supply chain issues.

While transitioning away from lead is taking time and is exacerbated by the shortage of copper bullets, it's important to underscore that a significant and growing number of hunters have willingly made the switch. The reasons that others have not yet transitioned to copper vary. Some hunters are unaware of the perils of lead, while others don't believe the science or think that switching from lead threatens their hunting traditions.

Nevertheless—someday—just as gasoline and paint containing lead are no more, lead bullets will also be a somber memory. But for now, the recovery program is playing a long game toward a lead-free future. Until the day arrives that lead bullets are no longer in use, they remain an ongoing danger to condors, other wildlife, and humans.

Condor biologists are also monitoring other environmental hazards including microtrash and DDT. Parent condors sometimes still bring microtrash to nest sites that can potentially cause problems if young chicks ingest it. And a new threat from DDT emerged that I covered in 2010. The source of the now-banned pesticide is a dump site off the Southern California coast that still contaminates ocean waters. The DDT accumulates in the food chain and can cause eggshell thinning in some condors feeding on marine mammals. That said, poisoning from spent lead ammunition remains the primary obstacle to the condor's full recovery.

○

On a May morning in 2022, two condors took flight from a new release site in Northern California that's a partnership between the Yurok Tribe and Redwood National Park. The release of the condors marked the first time in more than a century that America's largest bird has flown over the region's giant coast redwoods, the world's tallest trees. Located near the Oregon border, the site is working toward restoring condors to Yurok Ancestral Territory and the Pacific Northwest.

For thousands of years the fog-shrouded forests and salmon-filled rivers of this area have been the Yurok homeland. In 2003, tribal elders singled out the condor—*prey-go-neesh* in the Yurok language—as the highest-priority land-based animal to return to Yurok Ancestral Territory. The condor plays a significant role in the tribe's origin narrative as well as in the Yurok world renewal ceremonies that make use of the bird's feathers and songs. The Yurok Tribe partnered with Redwood National Park and lobbied and planned for years to develop the release site, which joins the previously established sites in Central and Southern California, Arizona, and Baja.

Later in 2022, the first pair of birds were joined by several more. Those condors sailing effortlessly above the lofty redwoods are a living manifestation of the Yurok's deep cultural bond to the birds. They represent another step toward restoring the biodiversity that prevailed before the Euro-American colonization of the area. Moreover, returning the condor to its role in maintaining intact ecosystems in the Pacific Northwest also enhances the spiritual lifeways of the region's tribes, who view the condor with reverence.

○

When I finished writing this Afterword early in 2023, I didn't imagine there would soon be another story to tell. But in the spring, the U.S. Fish & Wildlife Service reported concerning news: the first known cases of avian influenza in condors had killed three birds in Arizona. In addition, tests were being conducted on the bodies of five more condors also suspected of dying from the virus. And several sick condors were in quarantine and receiving medical care.

As we go to press at the beginning of June, here is what has happened thus far in the avian flu outbreak.

The first sign of trouble came in March when biologists observed a distressed female condor acting disoriented and lethargic. Initially, they presumed it was the usual culprit: lead poisoning. But when the bird died and they recovered her body, tests showed she had succumbed to Highly Pathogenic Avian Influenza (HPAI — pronounced "H-pie").

Avian influenza has infected North American domestic poultry as well as wild bird populations in the past. However, in January 2022 an especially contagious HPAI strain was identified in North American wild birds. Within a year it had spread across the continent, causing the largest avian flu outbreak on record.

Domestic poultry operations were also hit hard; to date, nearly 60 million farmed birds have died. Although HPAI mostly affects birds, the virus has also been found in some mammal species. Fortunately, the Centers for Disease Control and Prevention says that the currently circulating HPAI strain does not spread easily to people and the risk to humans is low.

Meanwhile, the number of infected Arizona condors mounted. Within days of the first confirmed cases, the U.S. Fish & Wildlife Service established an HPAI Incident Command Team to coordinate the response. In just over a month, twenty-one birds died, a loss of nearly 20 percent of the Arizona/Utah condor flock.

To everyone's relief, in mid-April the wave of condor infections in Arizona abated. However, recovery program partners remain on high alert. To date, there have been no cases in California or Baja, but preparations are underway if additional outbreaks occur, and the birds are being monitored closely for signs of illness.

Along with a pause in new infections, in May there was hopeful news from federal officials who granted emergency approval for an avian flu vaccine for condors. A trial to evaluate the vaccine's safety and effectiveness began immediately on black vultures, a relative of the condor. Assuming a good result, a second vaccine trial will then be conducted on a group of captive condors. If that trial also proves successful, vaccinations of wild and captive condors could begin.

No matter where this avian flu story leads, it accentuates the condor's vulnerability because of its small population and spotlights the urgency in finding a permanent solution to continual lead poisoning that is thwarting the bird's progress. A healthy wild condor population, unimpeded by these avoidable deaths from lead, helps clear the way for this remarkable species to better handle unexpected adversity and achieve full recovery.

○

In recent years, advances in technology have been a game changer. Improved wing-mounted GPS transmitters reveal more detailed information on where the birds are going and can even help in targeting nonlead outreach efforts. GPS tracking also shows the astonishing distances condors travel, with some birds clocking more than 1,500 miles in a single month.

In addition, with the now ubiquitous use of teleconferencing platforms such as Zoom, anyone can view a multitude of online offerings from different recovery program partners, chat with condor biologists, watch releases of new birds, stay up to date on condor news, and observe aspects of condor life that in the past only a few humans had been privileged to see.

My favorite technology is the wireless webcam. These small, solar-powered cameras livestream high-definition video and clear sound from remote condor nests and release pens. Early in 2020, the Ventana Wildlife Society installed a "condor cam" in a cavity in a huge redwood tree where their most experienced and productive Big Sur condor pair were likely to nest. Sure enough, in the spring the birds produced an egg, and the webcam allowed scientists and the public an intimate look at the two condors raising their chick.

With much of life shut down by the pandemic, I spent many happy hours in my writing studio in the company of those two condors caring for their baby chick, which I viewed on a separate monitor as I worked. Watching little Iniko, a Nigerian name meaning "born in troubled times," opened a window into another world. The tenderness between the birds as the baby nuzzled and played with her parents was palpable. You could hear the rustle of feathers while songbirds chattered nearby and feel the unhurried pace of the days as the birds followed the ancient rhythms of condor time.

But as spring turned to summer, wildfires started ravaging drought-stricken California. In August, with Iniko not yet able to fly, a blaze ignited in Big Sur and burned for weeks. One terrible night, webcams showed the conflagration raging through the condor sanctuary, engulfing the release pen and research facility. The video of the livesteam from Iniko's nest is hard to watch. You can hear the crackle and roar of the approaching flames, the fire casting flickering shadows in the redwood cavity as Iniko frantically flaps her wings in alarm. Embers sail through the night air. Then the video goes black, the webcam consumed by the inferno.

Two weeks passed before biologists could safely hike to Iniko's remote nest, hoping against hope for her survival. Iniko's redwood tree still stood amid the devastation, but the trunk had been scorched to within a few feet of the nest cavity. When biologists managed to peek inside, there she was, alive and well—a feathered miracle. Tragically, other birds were not so lucky. Eleven condors were lost to the flames that night, including one of Iniko's parents.

Increasingly frequent and destructive wildfires highlight the condor's consummate challenge: the turmoil from human-caused climate change, habitat destruction, and extinctions ravaging the planet. Global temperatures continue to arc relentlessly higher, with atmospheric CO_2 levels from burning fossil fuels now 50 percent above preindustrial times. In 2021, UN Secretary-General António Guterres called it "a code red for humanity."

When I wrote this book, the climate crisis appeared as a formidable but still distant storm. These days, the condor's range is beset with unprecedented droughts, heat waves, and wildfires—the sky has darkened, the climate crisis has arrived. We are living in what writer Kim Stanley Robinson calls "the emergency century."

The condor's struggles are echoed in the precipitous decrease in North American birdlife. Since 1970, we have lost a staggering three billion birds, more than a quarter of the continent's entire bird population. Over half of all U.S. bird species are in decline. Plummeting bird populations underscore the urgent need to address the threats to our avian brothers and sisters and the ecosystems they inhabit.

The condor's plight is just the tip of the feather.

Despite the daunting work that lies ahead for all of us, the condor program offers a touchstone for supporting other species as we navigate the turbulent waters of the environmental crisis.

○

It's early afternoon when we begin the return hike from the High Peaks, the chilly air punctuated by the rollicking calls of acorn woodpeckers. Condors have been an almost constant presence today—there are now five birds overhead. It's a comfort to watch them wheel and turn with graceful majesty. Despite all the obstacles and setbacks, including the years when the bird teetered on the very brink of the extinction abyss, condors are back in the skies where they have flown for millennia, back where they belong.

These five birds are a winged manifestation of the fierce dedication of so many people and the incredible work they have done—

and continue to do—to ensure the return of the condor, the return of *prey-go-neesh*. For those in the recovery effort, protecting these magnificent beings can be arduous: hiking into remote areas in all kinds of weather, absorbing the emotional toll of losing beloved birds to lead, and in some cases even putting their own lives at risk. This collaborative work embodies the best of humanity, an inspiration for changing our relationship with the natural world from subjugators to stewards.

As we make our way down the mountain, I'm filled with gratitude for the birds keeping us company. Eventually, the end of the trail comes into view, and I turn my eyes skyward a final time. The condors are now drifting toward the horizon, backlit by a gentle winter sun brightening the landscape with light and hope.

APPENDIX

The opportunity to view condors has never been better. As of 2023, free-flying condors can be seen in California, Arizona, and Utah as well as a remote location in Baja. Condors can also be viewed at several zoos. Here's how to identify a free-flying condor along with a listing from the U.S. Fish & Wildlife Service of the various California Condor Recovery Program partners.

CONDOR VIEWING TIPS

What to bring

Despite a condor's size, using a pair of binoculars will greatly enhance your viewing experience. A birder's spotting scope is also useful, although not essential.

A birding guide, such as *The Sibley Guide to Birds* by David Allen Sibley or the *National Geographic Field Guide to the Birds of North America*, can help you identify not only condors but also other birds as well. Phone apps such as Merlin are also useful.

Cautions

Biologists want condors to learn to avoid humans and human structures. You can help by not approaching wild condors. Maintain a good distance from the birds, speak in low tones, and keep your movements to a minimum. Do not feed condors, throw objects, or interact with them. If you see anyone harming or harassing a condor, please report it to the authorities. The condor is protected under the Migratory Bird Treaty Act and the Endangered Species Act.

Is it REALLY a condor?
A bird the size of a condor is easy to identify—once you know what to look for. To the unpracticed eye, however, flying condors can resemble other raptors. Experienced birders know that a bird's size—especially when it is flying in a distant sky—is not a reliable identification marker. Here are several identifiers that will enable you to say with certainty, "That's a condor!"

Ask: See that group of birders over there clustered around a spotting scope? Or a ranger or recovery team member? The odds are high that they will be happy to help you identify a bird.

Wing tags: All released condors carry highly visible number tags attached to the leading edge of one or both wings. The number tags are visible even when a bird is not flying. If you get a good look at a bird and don't see wing tags, it's most likely not a condor.

Flight pattern: Look for strong, steady flight. There's nothing uncertain about a condor's smooth soaring: it does not wobble or waver. The wings are held flat, and at their ends you'll see long flight feathers splayed out like giant fingers. Condors sometimes dangle their legs, especially when flying low.

Coloration: A mature condor has a black body and wings. On the leading edge of the underside of each wing is a striking, triangular white-patch. These wing patches are widest near the body and taper toward the wing tips. The bird also has an orange head and neck, although this may be hard to see at a distance. Newly released juvenile birds have dark heads and mottled white wing patches. As they mature, the adult coloration grows more distinct.

Size: Of course, the condor is gigantic. If you're lucky enough to be able to compare it with other birds, such as turkey vultures, there will be no doubt: condors look like small airplanes.

Similar birds that can resemble a condor
The ubiquitous turkey vulture is the bird most frequently confused with a condor. Even though its five-and-one-half-foot wingspan is almost half that of a condor, its soaring flight and similar coloration can cause uncertainty. Here's how to tell the difference:

"Tippy" flight: Soaring turkey vultures fly with an unsteady rocking motion. A large black bird in a distant sky with a "tippy" flight pattern is almost always a turkey vulture.

V-shaped wings: Unlike condors, which hold their wings flat, turkey vultures soar with their wings in a dihedral "V-shape."

Two-tone underwings: From a distance, turkey vultures look black with gray tones on the back edges of their wings' undersides.

The much rarer golden eagle is another bird sometimes confused with a condor. From a distance, golden eagles look dark. With a six-and-one-half-foot wingspan, it's still considerably smaller than a condor. And, of course, it won't have number tags.

WHERE TO VIEW CONDORS

Condors fly enormous distances. Recent GPS data show some birds traveling as much as 250 miles in a single day, and it's not unusual for birds to explore new areas as they look for nesting sites and food sources. With that in mind, the best places to see condors can change over time and even during different seasons of the year. Your best bet for up-to-date information on where to view wild free-flying birds is to visit the websites or contact the agency or entity in the region where you are planning to look. The California Condor Recovery Program is led by the U.S. Fish & Wildlife Service, and that's a good source of current information. Or contact the national park or nonprofit condor program partner in the geographic region in which you are interested.

Below are the 2023 recovery program partners and government and private entities listed by the USFWS.

U.S. Fish & Wildlife Service California Condor Recovery Program Partners

The California Condor Recovery Program is an international multientity effort, led by the USFWS, to recover the endangered California condor. Partners in condor recovery include the Peregrine Fund, Ventana Wildlife Society, National Park Service, San Diego Zoo, Los Angeles Zoo, Oregon Zoo, Santa Barbara Zoo, Chapultepec Zoo, Arizona Game and Fish Department, California Department of Fish and Wildlife, Utah Division of Wildlife Resources, Bureau of Land Management, U.S. Forest Service, the federal government of Mexico, the Yurok Tribe, and a host of other governmental and nongovernmental organizations.

U.S. National Parks where condors can be viewed include Redwood National Park, Pinnacles National Park, Grand Canyon National Park, and Zion National Park. In 2020, a group of six condors was seen for a short time in Sequoia National Park.

INDEX